THE STRUCTURE OF ENGLISH ORTHOGRAPHY

JANUA LINGUARUM

STUDIA MEMORIAE
NICOLAI VAN WIJK DEDICATA

edenda curat

C. H. VAN SCHOONEVELD

INDIANA UNIVERSITY

SERIES MINOR

NR. 82

1970

MOUTON

THE HAGUE · PARIS

THE STRUCTURE OF ENGLISH ORTHOGRAPHY

by

RICHARD L. VENEZKY

UNIVERSITY OF WISCONSIN

1970

MOUTON

THE HAGUE · PARIS

LIBRARY OF CONGRESS CATALOG CARD NUMBER: 73-98472

Printed in The Netherlands by Mouton & Co., Printers, The Hague.

To my wife

PREFACE

The work presented here is one result of a continuing analysis of the reading process, an analysis which originated at Cornell University as a component of what later became Project Literacy, was pursued at Stanford University as a dissertation project, and is continuing now at the Wisconsin Research and Development Center for Cognitive Learning. Central to all this work has been an attempt to understand what the reading process is and what is lacking in those children who have trouble learning to read. The first phase of this work, represented in part by the material presented here, was linguistic in nature, aimed towards an exhaustive description of the relationship between spelling and sound. The present work is derived mainly from my doctoral dissertation (1965), with additional material added from studies done in 1966. The second phase, in progress now, is more psychologically oriented. It began with the linguistic data obtained in phase one and proceeded to ask which of the posited letter-sound patterns are employed by competent readers, and how they are acquired. From this basis, the research has expanded into almost all areas of the reading process. Its original goal, however, has remained the same: to improve the teaching of reading.

This work, like most extensive research efforts, is not solely the product of one person, but drew upon the advice and criticism of a number of others. Foremost among these is Ruth H. Weir, whose tragic and untimely passing in November of 1965 deprived me of a friend and colleague and the academic world of an esteemed scholar. Her contribution to the study of English orthography is far in excess of what I can express here. Among the others to whom I am indebted are: Professors Harry Levin and E. J. Gibson of Cornell University whose encouragements helped sustain my interest in reading and whose own works have been models for my studies; Professor Charles Hockett of Cornell University who started me on the present course; and my wife whose contribution is much less specific than those listed above, but no less important.

R. L. V.

Tel Aviv, 1969

TABLE OF CONTENTS

I

PURPOSE, PLAN, AND SCOPE

> ... everyone ... has to admit that of all languages of culture English has the most antiquated, inconsistent, and illogical spelling.
>
> R. E. Zachrisson, 1930, p. 10.

1. INTRODUCTION

Educators, orthoepists, philologists and spelling reformers have from the darkest periods of the Middle Ages joined in the assault upon the 'antiquated', 'inconsistent', and 'illogical' spelling with which the English speaking world is burdened.[1] The Anglo-Saxons, working with an Irish-flavored Latin alphabet, established by the middle of the eleventh century orthographic practices consistent enough not only to serve their own needs, but also to serve as a basis for the Norwegian and Icelandic orthographies.[2] Norman invaders, however, carrying the orthography of the Continent, took immediately to reforming English spelling. New letters were introduced; old letters were discarded, and the entire system was endowed with an Anglo-Norman flavor. In time the Anglo-Norman language disappeared, but Anglo-Norman graphic practices had already become a permanent part of English spelling.

While the Anglo-Norman attack waned, a Latin assault on English orthography waxed. New words were imported with

[1] These descriptions of English spelling can be found in, among others, Hart (1551), Zachrisson (1930), Bloomfield (1933), and Lounsbury (1909).

[2] See George T. Flom, "Studies in Scandinavian Paleography", *JEGP*, 14 (1915), 530-43.

clean, Latin spellings; old words were redressed to parade their classical origins. But even though *t* was substituted for quite a few *c*'s and *s*'s, and some *b*'s and *h*'s were inserted where they didn't belong, the old system was still visible through the pale.[3] Sixteenth and seventeenth century grammarians, aroused by "the gros and disgrac'ful barbarismes" of the existing orthography, labored religiously to convert their countrymen to new spelling systems, but the ravages of conservatism and the relentless movement of time laid waste their proposals, leaving the banner for the Ben Franklins and the G. B. Shaws of the coming centuries.[4]

With the rise of comparative philology in the early nineteenth century, a new era of tranquility arose. Instead of scorn and contempt, dispassionate analysis was in vogue for the orthography. This romance, however, was short-lived. The Rasks and Grimms soon learned that the letters weren't really the sounds, and the orthography was relegated to the backporch of the new linguistic science. With structural linguistics came even harsher treatment. "Writing is not language" claimed one of the *dicta* of the new science, "but merely a way of recording language by means of visible marks", and the dust grew thicker, stirred into motion only by an occasional spelling reformer who sought rapid condemnation and execution for the prevailing orthography.[5] In recent years a new scientific interest in English spelling has arisen. Linguists, educators, and psychologists joined forces several years ago to investigate the reading process, and through their efforts a thorough study of English spelling-to-sound correspondences was begun.[6] In the resulting investigation, evidence was found to show that English spelling is more complex and contains a higher degree of patterning than was ever assumed before. From an interest in the nature and origins of the spelling patterns revealed by that study, the present work evolved.

[3] On the Latin influence in English orthography, see Venezky (1965), Chapter VII.

[4] Albert Eichler, *Charles Butler's English Grammar* (Halle, 1910), p. 16.

[5] Leonard Bloomfield, *Language* (New York, 1933), p. 21.

[6] See pp. 11-12.

2. PURPOSE

The function of this book is to show the patterning which exists in the present orthography — not just in terms of regular spelling-to-sound rules, but in terms of the more general phonemic and morphemic elements which characterize the system. For centuries philologists have approached the study of English orthography with the purblind attitude that writing serves only to mirror speech, and that deviations from a perfect letter-sound relationship are irregularities. Even so astute a scholar as Leonard Bloomfield added his authority to this view.

> Although our writing is alphabetic, it contains so many deviations from the alphabetic principle as to present a real problem, whose solution has been indefinitely postponed by our educators' ignorance of the relation of writing and speech.[7] ... The difficulty of our spelling greatly delays elementary education, and wastes even much time of adults. When one sees the admirably consistent orthographies of Spanish, Bohemian, and Finnish, one naturally wishes that a similar system might be adopted for English.[8]

Whatever may have been the relationship between writing and sound when the first Old English writings were inscribed in Latin script, and whatever may have been the reasons for the subsequent development of this system, be they due to random choice or to an all-pervading National Orthographic Character, the simple fact is that the present orthography is not merely a letter-to-sound system riddled with imperfections, but instead, a more complex and more regular relationship wherein phoneme and morpheme share leading roles. The synchronic study described here shows these different levels of patterning in the current orthography.

3. SOURCE MATERIALS

The main research upon which this book is based was begun at Cornell University in 1961. As part of the inter-disciplinary study

[7] Bloomfield, 1933, pp. 500-01.
[8] *Ibid.*

mentioned earlier a study of spelling-to-sound correspondence was undertaken by a group of linguists under the direction of C. F. Hockett. After an initial study of monosyllables (Hockett, 1961), a computer program was written to derive and tabulate spelling-to-sound correspondence in the 20,000 most common English words (Venezky, 1962).[9] This program was used by the author to obtain, for a corpus of the 20,000 most common words in English, the following information:

(1) A complete tabulation of the spelling-to-sound correlations found in the corpus, based upon the position of consonant and vowel clusters within the printed words. Thus, for any continuous string of vowels or consonants found in a printed word, the tabulations include all of the pronunciations found for that string, along with the totals and percentages for each pronunciation in each word-position (initial, medial, and final).

(2) Complete word lists for each correspondence found in (1) above. For example, if the cluster *gh* with the pronunciation /g/ occurred in 1 above, then the word list would contain all of the words in the corpus in which *gh* was pronounced /g/, arranged into separate, alphabetized lists for the three word positions.

(3) The same as (1) and (2) above for the 5,000 most common words in the corpus and for the graphic monosyllables.

(4) A dictionary of the corpus in which spellings were reversed and then alphabetized. This list was used extensively for studying suffixes and other word endings.[10]

Foremost among the published works used for this study was the *Oxford English Dictionary* (OED), the source for which the English language has yet to create an adequate superlative. The extent to which I am indebted to Messrs. Craige, Murray, *et al.*, for infor-

[9] This work was supported by U. S. Office of Education grants 639, OE-4-10-206 and OE-4-10-213.

[10] All of these data were compiled on the CDC 1604-A computer in Palo Alto, California.

mation on spellings, etymologies, and historical phonology is far in excess of the number of references to the *OED* in this book.

4. PLAN AND SCOPE

Previous analyses of English orthography, beginning with the sixteenth century spelling reform tracts, are surveyed in Chapter II. In Chapters III and IV the basis for the present analysis is presented, including a model for mapping from spelling into sound (Chapter III), and an analysis of the graphemic system (Chapter IV). In Chapters V and VI the model is applied to the consonant spellings (Chapter V) and the vowel spellings (Chapter VII); a short sketch of the morphophonemic system is presented in Chapter VI. In the final chapter I have outlined, among other conclusions, the implications of this study for the teaching of reading and for spelling reform.

The synchronic material presented here is based upon the spelling-to-sound correspondences which occur in the 20,000 most common English words, although words outside of this corpus are cited occasionally to illustrate interesting or unusual patterns.[11] Proper nouns, contractions, hyphenated words, and variant pronunciations of the same spellings are not included in this corpus. All pronunciations are based upon Kenyon and Knott, *A Pronouncing Dictionary of American English* (Springfield, Mass., 1951). Symbols employed for the pronunciation of Modern English are shown below.[12] Except where non-phonemic contrasts are discussed, these symbols are enclosed in slant lines, e.g., /e/. The same symbols are used between braces, e.g., {d}, to represent morphophonemic forms. Graphemic units are given in italics, e.g., *e*.

[11] In the *Thorndike-Century Senior Dictionary* the most common 20,000 words according to the Thorndike frequency count are identified. Many low-frequency words from that list, especially proper nouns, were omitted by the present writer, and a number of words not included in the original Thorndike list were included.

[12] See Hans Kurath, *A Phonology and Prosody of Modern English* (Ann Arbor, 1964), Chapter 1, for a discussion of the transcription system used here.

Vowels

checked vowels[13]		free vowels	
ɪ	b*i*t	i	b*ea*t
ɛ	b*e*t	e	b*ai*t
æ	b*a*t	ɔ	b*a*ll
a	b*o*p	o	h*o*me
ə	s*o*me	u	b*oo*t
ʊ	f*u*ll	aɪ	b*i*te
		aʊ	h*ow*
		ɔɪ	b*oy*

Consonants and Glides

p	*p*in	s	*s*in
b	*b*at	z	*z*ebra
t	*t*ip	š	*sh*in
d	*d*im	ž	rou*g*e
č	*ch*in	m	*m*at
ǰ	*j*ar	n	*n*et
k	*k*ick	ŋ	ri*ng*
g	*g*ate	l	*l*amp
f	*f*in	r	*r*ip
v	*v*at	w	*w*et
θ	*th*in	j	*y*et
ð	*th*en	h	*h*it

[13] The terms LONG and SHORT as applied in educational literature and in dictionaries to English vowel sounds are neither historically accurate nor mnemonically useful. While some of the Modern English long-short pairs have developed from Middle English vowels which supposedly differed only in quantity (commonly called length), this is certainly not true of all such pairs. Modern English long *u* (/ju/), for example, has developed primarily from /ü/ in French borrowings. Middle English long *u* (/ū/) has become MnE /au/ as in *house*. Anglo-Norman scribes imported the French spelling *ou* for ME /ū/ in the twelfth century, but left untouched the spelling *u* for short *u* (/u/), thus destroying for posterity a graphemic identity between the long and short *u* sounds and their reflexes in MnE. (The MnE sounds derived from ME long and short *u* are /au/ < /ū/ and /ʊ/ or /ə/ < /u/). In addition, MnE long and short *o* are not derived from their ME namesakes, but from ME /ɔ/ and /o/.

Long and short vowels are defined today in terms of spelling — they are the primary alternate pronunciations of the spellings *a*, *e*, *i*, *o* and *u*. The other

Schwa is used both for the stressed vowel as in *come* and the unstressed neutral vowel, as in the first syllable of *away*. To indicate the correspondences between graphemic, morphophonemic, and phonemic units, the abbreviations x → {y}, {x} → {y}, and {x} → /y/ are written. The arrow indicates that the unit on the left corresponds to the unit on the right. This is always to be interpreted as a one-way correspondence from left to right; correspondences in the other direction, that is, sound-to-spelling correspondences, are beyond the scope of this study. The urge to introduce more symbolic notation in the name of brevity or economy has been checked by the force of the following statement, made by Einar Haugen at a time when mathematics was still relatively foreign to linguistic disquisition.

> Present day descriptions bristle like a page of symbolic logic and lack entirely the leisurely, even charming quality of the traditional grammars. I would not go back to those grammars, but only suggest that economy may not always be a virtue. ...[14]

English vowels, however, seem to have no place in this scheme. How, for example, are /ɔ/ and /ʊ/ to be classed?

To answer this question by appeal to phonetic length is not justified by the classifications of the other vowel sounds. For two spellings, *a* and *o*, the long vowels are on the average phonetically shorter than the short ones (see Gordon E. Peterson and Ilse Lehiste, "Duration of Syllable Nuclei", *JASA* 32 (1960), 693-703). Furthermore, since vowel length varies according to the following sound, almost all long vowels are pronounced in some environments with durations which are shorter than the maximum durations of their corresponding short vowels.

A more theoretically accurate and educationally practicable nomenclature for English vowels is FREE and CHECKED. All stressed MnE vowels are either CHECKED or FREE; the unstressed vowel /ə/ forms a class by itself. "Checked vowels", according to Kurath, "do not occur at the end of morphemes; they are always followed by one or two consonants." (Kuruth, 1964, p. 17). Free vowels occur both in morpheme-final position and before consonants. (This distribution does not hold for final [a] forms like *ma* and *pa*, nor for the forms like *city* and *candy* when pronounced with a final [ɪ]). Furthermore, some free vowels are commonly articulated with prominent off-glides — /i, e, o, u/ (phonetically [ij, ej, ow, uw]) — or are diphthongal — /ai, au, ɔi/. Checked vowels are most often articulated as monophthongs; they may be in-gliding (phonetically [ɪᵊ, ɛᵊ]), but never off-gliding.

14 Einar Haugen, "Directions in Modern Linguistics", *Lg.* 27 (1951), 222.

II

ATTITUDES TOWARD ENGLISH ORTHOGRAPHY

1. INTRODUCTION

The earliest writings on English orthography are based upon an alphabetic principle derived from the fourth and sixth century Roman grammarians. Each letter of the alphabet has, besides its name (*nomen*) and appearance (*figura*), a power (*potestas*) or sound, and a description of the orthography involves simply a classification of the letters according to their powers.[1] Thus, orthography from the time of Alfred to the present day has been delimited by the letters and their powers. So ingrained has this principle become that some contemporary linguists have attempted, by substituting GRAPHEME for LETTER, to sanctify it with the countenance of linguistic science without examining how unsound it is.[2]

Some critical exceptions to this view are found in the writings of Francis (1958), Hockett (1958), and Vachek (1959). While all three of these have recognized that the orthography is more complex than an irregular letter-to-sound system, only Francis has attempted, with considerable success, to analyze the relationship between spelling and sound and to enumerate the non-phonemic elements which enter into this relationship. Most other linguists have paid little attention to the orthography. Bloomfield, for example, held that writing was not a part of language, but simply an imperfect image of speech, and even though he wrote at length

[1] See Einar Haugen, *The First Grammatical Treatise: The Earliest Germanic Philology* (Baltimore, 1950), pp. 41-2.

[2] The so-called grapheme-phoneme parallel is discussed on pp. 47-49.

on the teaching of reading, he maintained that English orthography was simply a grossly irregular alphabetic system.[3]

Spelling reformers, who have contributed an enormous quantity of literature on English orthography, have seldom analyzed the object of their scorn beyond the more common examples of scribal pedantry. Their arguments were, and are still, based upon the *a priori* assumption that alphabets should, and by some right ought, to be perfectly phonetic. It is no surprise, therefore, that most spelling reformers have concerned themselves with direct letter-to-sound relationships and have ignored all other facets of the writing system.

Grammarians, like the spelling reformers, have also viewed the orthography as a mirror for speech. The earliest grammarians concerned themselves primarily with correct pronunciation and, therefore, directed their attention towards relating spelling directly to sound. As spelling became regularized, they turned more and more toward establishing spelling rules, but still retained a direct spelling-to-sound standpoint. From the time of the earliest English grammars, however, a small number of grammarians have discerned non-phonetic features in the orthography, although few carried out comprehensive analyses of such features.

2. GRAMMARIANS

a. *Introduction*

Grammarians from the time of the earliest English grammars to the present time have generally shown little interest in orthography. The earliest treatments of spelling contain enumerations of the letters, based mostly upon the tri-partite system of Donatus (name, appearance, and force), and occasional statements on how the letters are to be pronounced. Prior to the sixteenth century, the only grammars written in English were restatements of Latin grammars based upon Donatus and Priscian, with little native

[3] See p. 11.

originality.[4] The revival of learning in the sixteenth century, however, brought a flood of literature on English grammar and consequently a greater interest in orthography. Coincidental with this phenomenon, the rise of printing hastened the regularization of spelling, and for the first time, spelling rules for English were formulated. By the eighteenth century spelling rules had become the center of discussions about orthography.

Most English grammarians prior to the twentieth century viewed spelling as a record of speech sounds, although some divergent views were expressed from time to time. Direct spelling-to-sound relationships form the basis of even the most enlightened treatments of the orthography, like those by Jespersen and Sweet.[5] Of these treatments of the orthography, three are especially significant for the present work; these are the works of Alexander Hume (c. 1617), James Douglas (c. 1740), and Goold Brown (1859).

Hume was one of the first grammarians to discuss orthographic practices and to explain such early Modern English innovations as the substitution of *t* for *c* and *s* in words of Latin origin like *nation* and *congregation*. Douglas was one of the few grammarians ever to attempt a complete description of English spelling-to-sound correspondences, and while his rules generally neglect nonphonetic features like morpheme identity, his results are as successful as any of the modern letter-to-sound descriptions. Brown, who published at least six different English grammars between 1820 and 1850, compiled in the *Grammar of English Grammars* the opinions of several hundred grammarians on various topics including the orthography. In what appear to be Brown's own contributions to the topic of orthography, the notion that spelling relates to something more than sound is advanced. Brown certainly did not view spelling as a direct reflection of speech, yet it

[4] See George L. Kittredge, "Some landmarks in the history of English grammars", *Text-book bulletin for schools and colleges* (N.Y., 1906), *passim*.

[5] Henry Sweet discusses the orthography in several sections of his *History of English Sounds From the Earliest Period* (Oxford, 1888). Jespersen was especially interested in the English orthography, yet approached it only from the sound-to-letter standpoint. See especially *A Modern English Grammar on Historical Principles* (Heidelberg, 1909-1931), I, 3.

is not clear what relation he postulated for spelling, sound and meaning. His writings are, nevertheless, significant for a survey of nineteenth century attitudes towards spelling, just as the works of Douglas and Hume are significant for attitudes of the previous centuries.

b. *Alexander Hume*

Alexander Hume's *Of the Orthographie and Congruitie of the Britan Tongue*, written around 1617, is one of the earliest English works in which spelling patterns are discussed.[6] Although born a Scotsman, Hume spent sixteen years in England, studying, teaching, and serving as schoolmaster at Bath. Upon returning to Scotland, he became rector of a high school and later, principal master of the grammar school of Dunbar, where he wrote the *Orthographie and Congruitie*, dedicating it to James I. This book was apparently designed as a spelling-book and grammar for use in the Dunbar schools. Hume also wrote a Latin grammar which was, by declaration of Parliament and the Privy Council, to be used in all the schools of the Kingdom. There is no evidence, however, that the injunction was carried out.

In the dedication to the *Orthographie and Congruitie* Hume noted the "uncertentie in our men's wryting", and claimed to have devised a "remedie for that maladie", which he said he put aside when he learned of Sir Thomas Smith's spelling-reform proposal (see page 30). The book itself is divided into two sections: "Of the orthographie of the Britan tongue" and "Of the congruitie of our Britan tongue". Spelling matters occupy approximately one-third of the first section, the remainder of this section being devoted to the sounds of the "Latine" and "Britan vouales" and "consonantes", and the syllable.

[6] The text has been edited by Henry B. Wheatley and published in the *EETS* Publication No. 5 (London, 1865). Some interesting remarks similar to Hume's can be found in Mulcaster's *Elementarie*, ed. E. T. Campagnac (Oxford, 1925), pp. 115ff. See also Eric J. Dobson, *English Pronunciation, 1500-1700* (Oxford, 1957), I, 316-21.

The basis of orthography according to Hume consists of "...the symbol, the thing symbolized, and their congruence". Congruence is "... the instrument of the mouth, quhelk, when the eie sees the symbol, utteres the sound". As for the symbols, he recommended that *i* and *u* be used only for vowel sounds and *j* and *v* only for consonants, and assigned the names *jod a*nd *jau* to the latter two. This separation was not widely adopted until almost 100 years later. It was not, for example, advocated in Ben Jonson's grammar which was published at least 15 years after the *Orthographie and Congruitie* was published.[7]

Two short chapters in the first Section of the *Orthographie and Congruitie* are devoted to spelling rules. The first, "of rules from the Latin", is interesting because it states a rationale for the Latin spellings which were adopted into English orthography during the sixteenth century.

> Heer, seeing we borrow miqkle from the latin, it is reason that we either follow them in symbolizing their's or deduce from them the groundes of our orthographie.[8]

Rule 2 of this chapter states that Latin derivatives written in Latin with *c*, *s*, or *sc* for /s/ should retain their original spellings. The distinction between *c* and *s* is especially important since "wordes of one sound and diverse signification are many tymes distinguished be these symboles". Hume cited such pairs as *council*: *counsil* and *cel* (*cell*): *sel* (*sell*). Latin verbals in *tio*, like *oration*, *visitation*, and *vocation* are to be written with the *t*, but "wordes deryved from the latin in tia and tium we wryte with ce; as justice, from justitia". Hume noted also that although the final *e* in justice "be idle, yet use hes made it tollerable to noat the breaking of the c." The other rules for Latin words deal with Latin *x* and with the vowels.

In the second spelling chapter, entitled "Of some idioms in our orthographie", Hume discussed, among less interesting topics, the symbolization of the syllabics /l̩/ and /ŋ̩/, and final *e*. Since "the

[7] Ben Jonson, *The English Grammar* (London, 1634).

[8] Hume, p. 19.

ear can hardlie judge quhither their intervenes a voual or noe" in the syllabic endings of "*litle, mikle, muttne, eatne*", he left to the "wil of the wryter" whether to write the *e* before the final consonant or after it. Hume rejected the idea that final *e* marks the quantity of a preceding vowel, because he did not believe that one vowel could change the sound of another if they were separated by a consonant.

... but it is as untrue that the voual e behind the consonant doth change the sound of the voual before it. A voual devyded from a voual be a consonant can be noe possible means return through the consonant into the former voual. ... Nothing can change the sound of a voual but an other voual coalescing with it into one sound. ...[9]

He did, however, approve of the final *e* to "break the sound" of *c* and *g* as in *peace* and *savage*, and after *s* as in *false* and *case*, for which he gave no reason. The *e* here is probably to show that *s* is pronounced /s/ rather than /z/, as it would be in *false* and *case* if the *e* were not present. As Wheatley pointed out in his notes to the E.E.T.S. edition of Hume's *Orthographie and Congruitie*, Hume's spelling itself is occasionally inconsistent. *Judge*, for example, is rendered alternately as *judge* (page 8), *juge* (page 18), and *judg* (page 33). Nevertheless, Hume's notes are valuable for what they reveal about the development of orthographic practices.

c. *James Douglas*

One of the more thorough treatises now in existence on English spelling-to-sound correspondences was written by James Douglas around 1740. Douglas, physician, anatomist, and fellow of the Royal Society, wrote, but never published, drafts of Latin, Greek, French and English grammars. The manuscripts are now housed in the Hunterion Museum, Glasgow, and a fragment on English orthography (H. M. 586), has recently been edited by B. Holmberg and published in *Lund Studies in English*.[10] In writing his treatise

[9] *Ibid.*, p. 21.

[10] Borje Holmberg, *James Douglas on English Pronunciation, c. 1740* (Lund, 1956). The most complete summary of direct spelling-to-sound correspondences is Axel Wijk's *Rules of Pronunciation for the English Language* (London, 1966).

on spelling-to-sound correspondences, Douglas attempted to record the upper-class speech of London. As a phonetician he was competent, but more important for the interests of this paper, he gave hundreds of rules for predicting sound from spelling and illustrated his rules with over 6,500 different words. The rules are based mostly upon the syllable position in the word and the letter position in the syllable. More sophisticated ideas, like those based upon accent position and morpheme identity are also used, but not frequently. Typical of his rules is "When the vowel A makes a compleat syllable in the beginning of a word, & is not a preposition, it is sounded long & slender, as, ... Ā-BLE. ..."[11]

Douglas attempted to use morpheme identity in some of his rules, but usually resorted to his favorite stand-by, syllable division, when nothing else worked. For example, *I* is long "in monosyllables before *Gn*, as SĪGN", and "in the first syllable of derivatives from monosyllables that are long, as ... SĪGNED." If DERIVATIVES is limited to a certain class of derivational and inflectional forms, this rule is valid. But for the final cluster *gn*, whose patterning can be derived from the rules for the *I* before it, Douglas resorted to syllable division, which in this case makes his rules either circular or useless.

> When gn closes the syllable in the middle of a word, the consonant G is not sounded, as ASSIGNEE. ... Whe G & N are divided into two syllables the consonant G is sounded hard, as ASSIGNATION.[12]

Douglas's rules are primitive. His selection of graphemic units is not based upon any discernible criteria; *ya*, *ye*, *wa*, *wi*, for example, are classed as diphthongs, and *awe*, *ewe*, *eye*, *way*, with numerous others, are classed as triphthongs. Furthermore, Douglas did not recognize the existence of /ŋ/, but rather, interpreted it as /n/ plus /g/. He also claimed that certain consonants were sounded double: "... the consonant B is sometimes sounded double, as, ... CABBIN."[13] The effects of certain consonant groups like *ld* and *ft* on preceding vowels are recognized, although the

[11] *Ibid.*, p. 128.
[12] *Ibid.*, p. 264.
[13] *Ibid.*, p. 233.

effect of accent on the pronunciation of intervocalic *x* is not. The merit of his work lies more in the intent than the results, although the 358 rules he presented, along with the lists of examples and exceptions, represent an extremely thorough attempt to analyze English spelling-to-sound correspondences.

d. *Goold Brown*

Goold Brown's *Grammar of English Grammars*, first published in 1850, is important both for what Brown himself says about orthography in remarks scattered over one thousand pages, and for the statements of the grammarians he cites.[14] The introduction of the *Grammar* contains the names of 548 grammatical works by 452 authors, including Aristotle's *Poetics* and the works of Bullokar (1586), Gill (1621), and B. Jonson (1634). An entire chapter is devoted to William Lily and Lindley Murray whose grammars were exceedingly popular in the middle of the nineteenth century. The section on orthography follows the traditional organization of letters, syllables and words, but includes a final section on spelling where such nineteenth century conflicts as those over final *c vs.* final *ck* and *our vs. or* are aired in full. To the graphemic triumvirate of NAME, APPEARANCE and FORCE Brown added CLASS, a distinction used by Donatus, but not placed on the same level as the other three properties. The two major classes of graphemic units are consonant and vowel, and consonants are further divided into semivowels and mutes. From this traditional introduction, Brown, in defining the powers of the letters, suggested that letters may relate to more than sounds.

> The deaf and the dumb, also, to whom none of the letters express or represent sounds, may be taught to read and write understandingly. ... Hence it would appear that the powers of the letters are not, of necessity, identified with their sounds; the things being in some respect distinguishable, though the terms are commonly taken as synonymous.[15]

Brown claimed to have had no interest in spelling reform as such,

[14] Goold Brown, *Grammar of English Grammars* (4th ed.; New York, 1859).
[15] *Ibid.*, p. 15.

but rather, in regularizing spelling. He summarized his observations on spelling with a plea for basing spelling on pronunciation, etymology, and "the analogy of the particular class of words to which it belongs". Some of his statements express quite sophisticated views on orthography, but there is insufficient evidence in his writings to determine what overall view he held about the orthography and whether the views he presented were his own or were summarized from other grammarians.

In his most progressive mood, Brown wrote that "words are not mere sounds, and in their orthography more is implied than in PHONETICS OR PHONOGRAPHY. Ideographic forms have, in general, the advantage of preserving the identity, history, and lineage of words...."[16] Brown's view is not unique; many of the early spelling reformers like Gill and Bullokar made similar statements. Unfortunately, Brown did not develop this idea further, and the only statement he made which bears directly on the question is shrouded in mysticism and retreat.

> In their definitions of vowels and consonants, many grammarians have resolved letters into *sounds only*. ... But this confounding of the visible signs with the things which they signify, is very far from being a true account of either. Besides, letters combined are capable of a certain mysterious power which is independent of all sound, though speech, doubtless, is what they properly represent.[17]

It is evident, nevertheless, that Brown wanted to separate writing from speech and avoid the confusions that arose in many earlier discussions of the subject. His spelling rules are nearly complete by modern standards, including such notes as "Monosyllables and English verbs end not with *c*, but with *ck* for double *c*"; moreover, his hints about the relationship of spelling to meaning foreshadow the writings of H. Bradley. Equally important are the citations from other grammarians on orthography, and the lengthy discussions on spelling disputes of the nineteenth century. The final *c vs. ck* (*music vs. musick*, etc.) controversy, for example, is pre-

[16] *Ibid.*, p. 203.
[17] *Ibid.*, p. 149.

sented with quotations from over twenty different British and American grammarians, including Lowth, Murray, Walker, Johnson, and Webster.

3. CONTEMPORARY LINGUISTS

The first twentieth century linguists were so adamant in pointing out the nineteenth century confusion of sound and spelling that they reduced the orthography to a secondary, subservient role from which it has infrequently emerged in the writings of contemporary linguists. The relationship between spelling and sound ranked high among the problems the first Indo-European comparative philologists faced. The early works of Bopp, Rask, and Grimm show classifications of sounds, based upon orthographic rather than phonetic data. On Bopp, F. de Saussure wrote "Even Bopp failed to distinguish clearly between letters and sounds. His works give the impression that a language and its alphabet are inseparable."[18]

Part of the early failure to distinguish clearly between phonology and orthography stemmed from the lack of an adequate vocabulary for discussing phonological phenomena. Grimm, for example, in *Deutsche Grammatik*, titled his discussion on sound changes "Changes of the letters". By the time of the publications of W. D. Whitney's *The Life and Growth of Language* (1874) and Hermann Paul's *Prinzipien der Sprachgeschichte* (1880), philologists had resolved most of the confusion between spelling and sound. Nevertheless, F. de Saussure inveighed against the orthography as the obfuscation of the true language. To Saussure are attributed the following remarks in the posthumous *Cours de linguistique générale*.

> Language and writing are two distinct systems of signs; the second exists for the sole purpose of representing the first. ... The preceding discussion boils down to this: Writing obscures language; it is not a guise for language but a disguise.[19]

[18] Ferdinand de Saussure, *Course in General Linguistic*, trans. Wade Baskin (New York, 1959), p. 10.
[19] *Ibid.*, pp. 23, 30.

To Saussure can also be attributed the first exposition on the so-called grapheme-phoneme parallel, a superficial relationship that is frequently invoked without critical comment by some contemporary linguists. Saussure saw four features in the letters (he did not use the term grapheme) which paralleled features in the phonemic system. His features, however, are equally applicable to morphemic and syllabic writing systems.

The phoneme-grapheme parallel has also been subscribed to by linguists since Saussure. Pulgram upped the count of parallel features to nine, including such items as the following:[20]

P 6 The phonetic shape of an allophone is dependent on its producer and on its phonetic surroundings	G 6 The graphic shape of an allograph is dependent on its producer and on its graphic surroundings
P 8 Dialects are subject to phonemic change and substitution	G 8 Alphabets are subject to graphemic change and substitution

Stetson in a brief note on phoneme and grapheme claimed that to understand written forms, one must understand writing movements, just as, apparently, one must understand articulatory movements to understand spoken forms.[21] Bazell, disagreeing with Pulgram in particular, objected to the phoneme-grapheme parallel on the grounds that phonemes contain simultaneous distinctive features while graphemes contain non-simultaneous ones.[22] Bazell's solution is that "the letter ... answers to the morpheme...." More recent renditions of the phoneme-grapheme parallel can be found in the writings of Francis (1958), Gleason (1961) and Hall (1964).

Considerations of the orthography by linguists, from the time of Saussure through the second World War, were directed mostly towards spelling reform. Many scholars who demonstrated adept-

[20] Ernst Pulgram, "Phoneme and Grapheme: A Parallel", *Word* 7 (1951), 15-20.

[21] Raymond H. Stetson, "The Phoneme and the Grapheme", *Melanges de linguistique et de philologie offerts à Jacq. Van Ginneken* (Paris, 1937).

[22] C. E. Bazell, "The Grapheme", *Litera* 3 (1956), 43.

ness and unbiased critical ability in all other phases of linguistic investigation could, in their passion for reforming English spelling, see nothing in the prevailing orthography except a defective alphabetic system, badly in need of repair. Bloomfield (see page 11) is responsible probably more than any other contemporary linguist for the view that writing is secondary and subservient to speech. This notion was espoused not only in *Language*, but also in several later articles.[23] Not all linguists in this century, nevertheless, held this view, and some, like H. Bradley who was cited earlier (see page 24) even claimed that writing does not attempt to relate directly and solely to speech. In commenting on graphic distinctions of homophones, Bradley stated

> It is because the expression of meaning is felt to be the real purpose of written language that these distinctions still survive, in spite of the disasterous effects that they have had on the phonetic intelligibility of written words.[24]

In summarizing his views on writing and speech, Bradley stated further that "speech and writing are two organs for the expression of meaning, co-ordinate and mutually independent".[25]

A more succinct summary of this relationship was made by C. F. Hockett in 1958:

> The complexities of English spelling cannot be accounted for completely on the assumption that the system is phonemic with irregularities of the sort listed ... [above]. It is necessary to assume that the system is partly phonemic and partly morphemic.[26]

This view was also expressed in 1941 by Edgerton in direct reply to Bloomfield's idea that writing relates only to speech. "Writing consists in the conventional use of visible symbols for the recording or transmission of ideas, or of ideas and sounds ... or of sounds unaccompanied by ideas."[27]

[23] See especially "Linguistics and Reading", *The El. Eng. Rev.* 19 (April, 1942), 125-130, 19 (May, 1942), 183-86.

[24] Bradley, 1928, p. 176.

[25] *Ibid.*, p. 186.

[26] Charles F. Hockett, *A Course in Modern Linguistics* (New York, 1958), p. 542.

[27] William F. Edgerton, "Ideograms in English Writing", *Lg.* 17 (1941), 149.

The Czech linguist Joseph Vachek has advanced, in a series of articles over the past thirty years, one of the most critical analyses of the English spelling-to-sound relationship. Vachek first distinguished the aims of the traditional writing system of a language from its phonetic transcription.

> While any system of phonetic transcription provides means for an optical recording of the purely acoustic make-up of spoken utterances, the traditional writing system increasingly tends to refer to the meaning directly without necessarily taking a detour via the corresponding spoken utterance.[28]

He then went on to give definitions of the spoken and written norms of language and to develop, in a general fashion, the hierarchic relation of the two norms of English.

Francis, in enumerating the nonphonemic features of English writing, pointed out not only the graphemic differentiation of homophones, but also the use of graphemic markers to show the phonemic correspondences of other graphemes, and the general tendency in English spelling to preserve morphemic identity regardless of phonemic differences.[29] Francis's most important result is the following:

> We may state this in terms of a general principle which, while admitting many exceptions, is what governs and systematizes many of the apparent inconsistencies of our wiiting system: The English writing system tends to employ a single combination of graphemes to represent a given morpheme, disregarding for the most part all except the grossest phonemic differences between allomorphs.[30]

Several twentieth century linguists have written on spelling-to-sound correspondences with the intent of improving the teaching of reading. Bloomfield, who condemned the orthography to eternal purgatory in *Language*, wrote several articles on the teaching of reading and in collaboration with Barnhart wrote an introduc-

[28] Josef Vachek, "Two Chapters on Written English", *Brno Studies in English*, I, 8 (Praha, 1959), see also Josef Vachek, "Some remarks on Writing and Phonetic transcription", *Acta Linguistica* 5 (1945-49), 86-93.

[29] W. Nelson Francis, *The Structure of American English* (New York, 1958), pp. 450-69.

[30] *Ibid.*, p. 468.

tory reading text.[31] Bloomfield published nothing on spelling-to-sound correspondences themselves. What notions he had on patterning in the orthography, judging from his published works, were based upon direct letter-sound relationships.

Another linguist who has written on reading is C. C. Fries, who set forth his views recently in *Linguistics and Reading*.[32] Fries brings to this task not only the tools of an eminent scholar, as did Bloomfield, but also those of an educator who has worked for over a half century in language teaching. His views on spelling-to-sound correspondences, however, are adapted for classroom application and consequently are non-technical in the linguistic sense. Only direct spelling-to-sound relations are mentioned, although the single-letter to single-sound correspondence has been replaced by the SPELLING PATTERN that corresponds as a whole to a sound or sequence of sounds. Forms like the final *e* in *like* are not seen as markers, but as parts of a larger, somewhat indefinite, spelling pattern. Morphemic elements are totally neglected as are all other non-phonetic influences.

> Modern English spelling is fundamentally a system of a comparatively few arbitrary contrastive sets of spelling patterns, to which readers, to be efficient, must, through practice, develop high-speed recognition responses.[33]

In contrast to this, Francis, who acknowledged both phonemic and morphemic elements in the orthography, considered the recognition of morphemic elements as important as the recognition of phonemic ones.

> Efficient reading is really a combination of two skills, both of which must be taught by any satisfactory method of teaching reading. They are, first, the ability to recognize accurately a large number of words and word groups as wholes ... and second, the ability to work out the pronunciation of an unrecognized graphic configuration, in terms of its constituent phonograms and morphograms, until it is recognized as a unit of the spoken vocabulary.[34]

[31] Leonard Bloomfield, 1933, 1942; L. Bloomfield and C. L. Barnhart, *Let's Read, a Linguistic Approach* (Detroit, 1961).

[32] Charles C. Fries, *Linguistic and Reading* (New York, 1962).

[33] *Ibid.*, p. 183.

[34] Francis, 1958, p. 558.

4. SPELLING REFORMERS

The literature on spelling reform is imbued with a revivalistic quality; it sees the prevailing orthography as the degenerate product of neglect, denseness, and lack of adaptability. It sees the future of the English speaking people, if this malignancy is allowed to remain, as continued degeneration: children failing to learn to read, adults falling prey to the corrupted speech of the lower classes, world trade falling off, and business suffering throughout the land. Nevertheless, from the *Ormulum* to the recent Initial Teaching Alphabet, spelling reformers, either covertly or overtly, have advanced theories of writing and notions about the relationship of spelling and sound.

The orthography of Orm, preserved in a holograph manuscript written around 1200 (*The Ormulum*) is the earliest remaining example of English spelling reform.[35] The orthographic regularity in this manuscript is unmatched until well after the introduction of printing and shows, among other things, an attempt to indicate vowel quantity through consonant doubling and accent marks. As a spelling reformer, he is both clumsy and dull, but as an indicator of concern for spelling-to-sound correspondences in the thirteenth century, Orm is unique. We can only assume from observing the form and regularity of Orm's spelling system, that he had spent some time analyzing the relationship between spelling and sound and had done so from a pure letter-sound basis. If Orm advocated a general spelling reform, then he failed. The text of the *Ormulum* is the only evidence we have of Orm's spelling system.

From the time of the *Ormulum* until the middle of the sixteenth century, we have no evidence of spelling reform attempts. Then, suddenly, in England spelling reformers flourished. Sir Thomas Cheke and Sir Thomas Smith, co-defendants in the great Greek controversy of the sixteenth century, were the first, followed closely by John Hart, the most competent by far, and then by an

[35] Bodleian Ms. Junius 1. See also R. W. Burchfield, "The Language and Orthography of the Ormulum MS", *Trans. Phil. Soc.* (1956), 56-87.

endless succession of others up to the present day. Most of the spelling reformers viewed writing as a mirror for speech, but a few like Bullokar and Gill proposed alphabets based at least in part upon etymology and upon the desire for a graphic distinction of homophones, and recognized non-phonemic elements in the orthography.

The earliest sixteenth century spelling reformers, Sir Thomas Cheke and Sir Thomas Smith, did not wage reform campaigns. That Cheke was interested in spelling reform is known only from his translation into a reformed English alphabet of the Gospel according to St. Mark (c. 1550), and from a letter he wrote to Sir Thomas Hoby, which was published in 1561.[36] Except for the symbol ω which he substituted for the spelling *oo*, Cheke employed only Latin letters, using, among other devices, geminate vowels to show quantity, geminate consonants to show a preceding short vowel, and *sch* for /š/. Although inconsistent in the employment of his orthography, Cheke attempted to devise a phonetic transcription system, as did Smith who saw writing only as the imitation of speech. Smith published his views on spelling reform in *De recta & emendata linguae anglicae* (1568), but did not advocate a particular spelling system. Rather, he offered variant spellings for the writer to choose from.[37] Smith worked from sound to spelling, employing at least thirty-four unique letter-forms along with the diaeresis, circumflex and hyphen.

John Hart was the most competent phonetician of the early reformers and also the most evangelistic. He saw in the orthography the vices of "diminution" (lack of enough letters), "superfluity" (use of superfluous letters), "usurpation by one letter of the powers of another", and "misplacement of letters" (failure of the order of the spelling to correspond to the order in which the letters are pronounced). In three major works published between 1551 and 1570, Hart enumerated and then vanquished the arguments against spelling reforms, set forth a reformed alphabet based entirely upon the existing Latin alphabet, and transcribed some

[36] See Dobson, 1958, I, 38-46.
[37] *Ibid.*, 46-62.

popular texts in his system.[38] Although his system is more consistent than those which followed him in the next two centuries, his chief value today is in the record he left of the speech of his time. While claiming that writing "is to leave a record of our thoughts", Hart could see no other way to achieve this goal than to write phonetically.

The major spelling reformers who followed Hart contributed little to the understanding of attitudes toward writing and the relation between writing and speech. While some of the later reformers based their systems upon etymology and analogy (see especially James Elphinstone) the majority advocated phonetic systems, and cited, to establish a need for reform, the same worn-out examples of scribal pedantry like *debt*, *doubt*, and *victuals*.

Beginning with the Spelling Reform Association which was founded in Philadelphia in 1876, various societies have been formed to further the spelling reform cause. Before the end of the Second World War the Anglic Association, the Simplified Spelling Society, the British Spelling Reform Association, the Simplified Spelling League and the Simplified Spelling Board organized, published manifestoes and occasional periodicals, and faded from existence. Within the ranks of these ephemeral societies, nevertheless, were counted such scholars as W.A. Craigie, A.J. Ellis, C.Grandgent, D.Jones, G.Krapp, G.Murray, and R.Zachrisson. The twentieth century reformers have in general presented an even more distorted picture of the orthography than their predecessors. Their arguments, instead of being based on the true irregularities which exist, generally are based upon non-existent patterns like the celebrated *ghoti* for /fɪš/ or upon renderings like the following:

> If one used all possible combinations, the word *scissors* ... might be spelt in 596,580 different ways. Dr. G. Dewey ... has calculated that the word foolish, if dealt with in the same way, might be spelt in 613,975 different ways.[39]

[38] Hart's three works have been edited by Bror Danielsson in *John Hart's works on English Orthography and Pronunciation* (Stockholm, 1955).

[39] R. E. Zachrisson, "Four Hundred Years of English Spelling Reform", *Studia Neophilologica* 4 (1931), 5.

A recent spelling reform revival has taken place in this country and in England, led by Sir James Pitman, the grandson of the inventor of the Pitman shorthand system.[40] While the earlier spelling reformers advocated complete and irreversible reform, Pitman has limited his interests to an Initial Teaching Alphabet (ITA) for use in the teaching of reading. Once adequate skill in reading in ITA is gained, the reader is transferred to conventional orthography.[41] The British government is sponsoring experiments with ITA in the British primary schools, and a number of American schools have either experimented with the system or have expressed a desire to do so. While the immediate results of experiments with ITA have been successful according to the proponents of the system, few critical analyses of the experiments or their results have been published.

[40] Isaac J. Pitman, "Learning to read: An Experiment", *J. Royal Society of Arts*, 109 (1961), 149-180.

[41] See John Downing, "Pitman's Initial Teaching Alphabet", Report given to the Conference on Perceptual and Linguistic Aspects of Reading (Stanford, 1963).

III

PRELIMINARIES TO ORTHOGRAPHIC ANALYSIS

1. GRAPHEMIC FEATURES

a. *Spelling Units*

Even from the direct letter-to-sound standpoint the graphemic system is more complex than is revealed in the notion that there are twenty-six letters, or graphemes, which through careful manipulation, are mapped into the phonemes of English. From the enumeration of the twenty-six graphemes to the point where correspondences to phonemes can be considered, a number of complexities must be untangled. One is the designation of the spelling units themselves. Obviously, there are more than twenty-six functional units; *th*, *ch*, and *oo*, for example, are as basic to the current orthography as *a*, *b* and *t*. But are *tch*, *ck*, and *dg* primitive units, on a level with *a* and *th*, or are they in some sense compound units, whose correspondences to sound can be predicted from their immediate constituents?

If spelling can be mapped into sound, then regardless of the intermediate levels which are introduced, graphemic words must be segmented into their basic graphemic units. This requires that there be some way of handling letters like the final *e* in *rove* and the *b* in *debt*. Is, for example, the *e* in *rove* connected to *o*, forming the discontinuous unit *o...e*, or is it part of the unit *ve*, or is it a unit by itself? And, similarly, how is the *b* in *debt* to be handled? As part of the unit *eb*, or of *bt*, or as a separate unit? The solution to this problem should not only be consistent with the way similar graphemes are handled, but also general enough to handle new cases which may arise. The designation of spelling units in *Webster's New Collegiate Dictionary*,[1] for example, fails to meet both of these aims. The editors give no general rules for handling silent letters, but instead haphazardly and quite inconsistently classify individual cases as they arise in traversing an alphabetical list of spelling units. *gh*, for example, "in *aghast*, *ghostly* and *ghost* is a useless spelling for 'hard' *g*. ..."[2] *rh*, however, as in *rhetoric* and *rhesus* is not mentioned as a separate unit. *ng* is a single unit in words like *long*, corresponding to /ŋ/, but *mb*, on the other hand, is two units, the second being silent.

These problems cannot be settled satisfactorily by simply labeling all unpronounced letters as silent. Consider the so-called silent *b*'s in *subtle* and *bomb*. One could say as *Webster's* does, that the *b*'s in these two words are silent, and let the matter rest. But by doing so, an important difference that exists in these two cases would be neglected. The form *subtle* occurs only with the *b* corresponding to zero, but *bomb* in *bombard* and *bombardier* has non-silent *b*. It is not sufficient therefore to say that the second *b* in *bomb* is silent; the more exact statement is that it is silent before word juncture and before certain suffixes (cf. *bombing*, *bombs*, *bombed*). This is one of the forms of orthographic patterning that almost all traditional treatments of spelling overlook. Its full implications are explored in a later section of this work.

Another inherent feature in the orthography is the distinction between functionally simple and functionally compound consonant units. One of the most general, although not entirely regular, spelling-to-sound rules is that the vowel spellings *a*, *e*, *i*, *o*, *u* are mapped into one form before a single consonant unit which is followed by a vowel and into another form in all other environments. In the vocabulary of the direct letter-to-sound school, these forms are the LONG and SHORT pronunciations of the vowels,

[1] John P. Bethel (ed.), *Webster's New Collegiate Dictionary* (2d ed., Springfield, Mass., 1956).
[2] *Ibid.*, p. xii.

as shown in the examples below (FREE and CHECKED in the vocabulary used here — see page 14).

	free pronunciation	checked pronunciation
a	/e/	/æ/
	*a*nal	*a*nnals
	*a*che	r*a*tchet
e	/i/	/ɛ/
	f*e*tal	f*e*ttle
	*e*ther	h*e*dge
i	/aɪ/	/ɪ/
	h*y*po	h*i*ppo
	wr*i*the	wh*i*ttle
o	/o/	/a/
	ph*o*nograph	s*o*nnet
	k*o*sher	n*o*xious
u	/(j)u/	/ə/
	s*u*per	s*u*pper
		l*u*xury

To apply this rule, simple and compound consonant units must be differentiated, a task which cannot be done by simply counting the number of letters involved. *sh*, for example, is composed of two letters, yet it functions as a simple unit as in *kosher*. *x*, on the other hand, contains only one letter, yet it functions as a compound unit, as in *luxury* and *noxious*. What must be formulated is a consistent criterion for classing consonant units as simple or compound. While the classifications of *x*, *ch*, *th*, *ph*, and *rh* may be intuitively obvious, those of *ck*, *dg*, and *tch* are not. What is important is first that, the rule mentioned above, and, as will be shown soon, almost all spelling-to-sound rules, be based not upon letters or graphemes as such, but rather upon functional spelling units, and second, that functionally simple and functionally compound units be distinguished.

b. *Graphemic Alternations*

A feature of the graphemic system which has arisen partially from scribal necessity and partially from pedantry is the alternation of various letters according to their graphemic environments. In such cases two different letters which correspond to the same sound occur in complementary (or near-complementary) distribution. The functionally simple vowel spellings *i* and *y*, for example, alternate, *y* occurring generally in final position and *i* in all other positions. In addition, regular rules control the alternation of final *y* to *i* before certain suffixes (see page 59). This alternation holds not only for the simple vowel spellings *i* and *y*, but also for the compound spellings in which these two letters occur as the second elements, e.g., *ai, ay, ei, ey*. In the compound units, the *y* spellings generally appear before other vowel spellings and in morpheme final position, and the *i* spellings appear in all other positions. For example, *bait*:*bay*, *heinous*:*grey*, *boisterous*:*boy*.

u and *w*, when each corresponds to /w/, also occur in complementary distribution. As a simple consonant spelling, *u* occurs in a limited number of environments: after *q*, *g*, *s*, and a few others — in all other cases *w* occurs. As second units in compound vowel spellings, *u* and *w* alternate similarly to *i* and *y*. Thus, *w* occurs as the second element before other vowel spellings and in morpheme final position, while *u* occurs in all other positions, e.g., *auction*:*awe*:*draw*; *feud*:*ewer*:*flew*; *ounce*:*coward*:*vow*.

Several other alternation patterns of lesser significance should also be considered in an exhaustive analysis of the graphemic system.

These patterns are listed below.[3]

(1) *ous*/*os* Word final *ous* becomes *os* before the suffix *ity*, e.g., *curious*:*curiosity*.

[3] On these patterns, see further, pp. 59-62.

(2) *i/e* — *i* in the suffix *ity* becomes *e* when the suffix is preceded by *i*, e.g., *society, variety, sobriety.*

(3) *er/re* — With the addition of certain suffixes, word final *er* becomes *re* and then the *e* is dropped; thus, *center*:*central*; *theater*:*theatrical.* In addition, *er* and *re* are in complementary distribution in word final position. *re* occurs after *c* and *g*, and *er* occurs in all other positions.

(4) Consonant gemination — Gemination of a final consonant occurs before certain suffixes, e.g., *run*:*running*, *hop*:*hopped.*

(5) *e/ø* — Final *e* alternates with zero under certain types of suffixation. Thus, *dive*:*diving*.

In addition to these alternations, a number of graphemic substitutions, introduced mostly between the times of Chaucer and Shakespeare, must be treated separately. One of these is the substitution of *t* for *c* in suffixes like *tion* and *tial*, e.g., *nation, essential* (cf. ME, *nacion, essenciall*). Early Modern English scribes, instilled with the fervor of classical learning, brought about in these substitutions one of the few true spelling reforms in English orthographic history. Their notion of reform, however, was to restore the appearance of the Latin root in favor of a more phonemic spelling. Another graphemic substitution was the early Modern English replacement of *u* with *o* in the vicinity of *m, n, u* (*v*). This substitution accounts for many of the so-called irregularities like *some, love,* and *ton.*[4] All of these alternations and substitutions are parts of the current orthography and must be considered in a description of orthographic patterns.

[4] "In ME texts of a more recent date (Chaucer, etc.) we find *o* used still more extensively for /u/, namely in the neighborhood of any of the letters *m, n,* and *u* (*v, w*). The reason is that the strokes of these letters were identical, and that a multiplication of these strokes, especially at a time when no dot or stroke was written over i, rendered the reading extremely ambiguous and difficult ... this accounts for the present spellings of won, wonder, worry, woman ... above, love ... and many others." Otto Jespersen, 1909, III, 482.

2. CORRESPONDENCES

Having pursued the graphemic labyrinth through its intra-graphemic complexities, the next task is to analyze the relationships of these units to sound. The object here is to show that even if the direct spelling-to-sound view is assumed, more types of relationships must be considered than the simple regular-irregular classes that bisect the traditional approach to this subject. Furthermore, it will be shown that the concepts of regular and irregular are far more complex than is generally assumed, and, indeed, require quite sophisticated notions for adequate definition. For the present, however, I will use 'regular' and 'irregular' in a loose sense, meaning simply, high frequency and low frequency, without careful enumeration of what objects are to be counted to arrive at such statistics.

Regular spelling-to-sound correspondences can be classed first as either INVARIANT or VARIANT. *f*, for example, corresponds regularly to /f/. In fact, this correspondence is so regular that only one exception, *of*, occurs among the 20,000 most common English words. Several other consonant spelling units like *ck*, *m*, *y*, and *z* are also invariant or nearly so. The vowel spellings, which are described in Chapter VI, (though not from the direct spelling-to-sound view), are rarely invariant, though not IRREGULAR in most cases.

Variant correspondences are those correspondences that are still regular, but that relate the same spelling to two or more pronunciations, depending upon graphemic, phonological, or grammatical features. Initial *c*, as an example, corresponds to /s/ when it occurs before *e*, *i*, *y*; in all other positions it corresponds to /k/. The spelling *k* corresponds to zero in initial position before *n*, e.g., *knee*, *know*, *knife*. In all other positions, *k* corresponds to /k/. This is graphemic conditioning from the letter-sound standpoint. As will be shown later, the silent initial *k* is explained more adequately by phonotactical rules. (The cluster /kn/ does not occur within a single morpheme in English; where such prohibited consonant clusters would otherwise occur in morpheme-initial position, the first consonant is dropped. Thus *knee*, *gnat*, *ptarmigan*, *pneumonia*, *psychology*).

Position alone may determine the correspondence of a spelling unit. For example, initial *gh* always corresponds to /g/: *ghost*, *gherkin*, *ghoul* (but never to /f/ as assumed in the spelling reform creation *ghoti*), but medial and final *gh* have pronunciations besides /g/, as is too often pointed out in spelling reform tracts. Stress may also be a conditioning factor for regular, variant correspondences. The most prominent role that stress plays in spelling-to-sound correspondences is in the pronunciation of unstressed vowels. While the reduction of unstressed vowels to schwa is not entirely regular, it can still be predicted in many cases. The patterns, however, are highly complex and are beyond the scope of this paper. A more interesting example of stress conditioning occurs in the correspondences for intervocalic *x*, which corresponds either to /ks/ or /gz/, depending upon the position of the main word stress. If the main stress is on the vowel preceding *x*, the pronunciation generally is /ks/ as in *exit*, *exercise*. Otherwise, the pronunciation is /gz/ (cf. *examine*, *exist*). While this rule is similar to Verner's Law for the voicing of the Germanic voiceless spirants, it is not a case of pure phonological conditioning. Words like *accede* and *accept* have the identical phonetic environments for /gz/, yet have /ks/.

Another type of correspondence in which stress is important is the palatalization of /sj, zj, tj, dj/ to /š, ž, č, ǰ/. This form of palatalization occurs when /sj, zj, tj, dj/ are followed by an unstressed vowel, as in *social*, *treasure*, *bastion*, and *cordial* (see Chapter VI).

The retention or deletion of medial /h/ in most cases also depends upon the position of the main word stress. Compare *prohibit*: *prohibition*; *vehicular*: *vehicle*. In each pair, the first member, which has the stress on the vowel following *h*, has a fully pronounced /h/, while the second member, with an unstressed vowel after *h*, has no /h/. This rule also holds for *vehement*, *shepherd*, *philharmonic*, *annihilate*, *rehabilitate* and *nihilism*, all of which generally have silent /h/. (Some forms like these may have /h/ occasionally preserved by over-correct pronunciations).

Irregular spelling-to-sound correspondences also show important differences. *Arcing* and *cello*, for example, both have irregular correspondences for *c*, yet there is an important distinction between these two irregularities. *Arc*, from which *arcing* is derived, has the correct correspondence for *c*. When suffixes beginning with *e, i, y* are added to words ending in *c*, a *k* is normally inserted after the *c*, as in *picnicking* (cf. *picnic*) and *trafficked* (cf. *traffic*). The irregularity in *arcing*, therefore, is in the irregular formation of the derivative. *Cello*, on the other hand, contains an aberrant correspondence for *c*, paralleled by only a few other Italian borrowings.[5] In the examination of the influence of morphemic features upon spelling-to-sound correspondences which follows, even more patterning appears, even though the direct letter-sound approach shows only irregularities.

3. MORPHEMIC FEATURES

a. *Morpheme Boundaries*

If the investigation of morphemic features is begun with the assumption of a direct relationship between spelling and sound, then problems appear immediately. The spelling *ph*, for example, regularly corresponds to /f/ as in *phase*, *sphere*, and *morpheme*. In *shepherd*, however, *ph* clearly does not correspond to /f/, but to /p/. One way to explain this is to say that *shepherd* is an exception to the more general rule of *ph* — /f/. But if this is done, then the same process must be repeated when faced with *uphill*, *topheavy* and every other form in which *ph* occurs across a morpheme boundary. The most satisfactory procedure is to say that *ph* corresponds to /f/ when it lies within a single graphemic allomorph and that across morpheme boundaries *ph* is treated as the separate

[5] *Concerto* and proper nouns like *Cellini* are the most common examples.

letters *p* and *h*. Therefore, one factor that should be considered in the spelling-to-sound relationship is morpheme boundaries. That this factor is not unique to *ph* can be seen from the following examples.

(1) Within graphemic allomorphs geminate consonant clusters (as in *letter*, *add*, and *canned*) are pronounced as single consonants. Across morpheme boundaries, however, both graphemic consonants may correspond to separate phonemes, as in *midday* and *finally*.

(2) All of the digraph and trigraph spellings are subject to the same morpheme boundary problem as *ph*, e.g., *hothead*, *changeable*.

(3) The spelling *n*, before spellings in the same morpheme which correspond to /g/ or /k/ corresponds to /ŋ/, as in *congress*, *finger*, *anchor*. Across morpheme boundaries this generally does not hold, e.g., *ingrain*, *ingenious*, *ingratiate*.

(4) Many word final clusters contain silent letters, e.g., *gm*, *gn*, *mb* (*paradigm*, *sign* and *bomb*). Across certain morpheme boundaries, the silent letter remains silent, as in *paradigms*, *signer*, and *bombing*. As long as the morpheme boundary is recognized, the correct pronunciation can be predicted. If the morpheme boundary is not recognized, then the three forms above would be thrown together with *stigma*, *ignite*, and *bamboo*.

In some cases the discrimination of a morphemic spelling from an identical, non-morphemic spelling is necessary for the prediction of sound from spelling. Consider the following two word lists.

A	*B*
boys	*melodious*
judges	*stylus*
cats	*apropos*
man's	*careless*

The pronunciation of final *s* in any column A word can be predicted by the following rules (these rules must be applied in the order shown here):

(1) /ɪz/ after /s, z, č, ǰ, š, ž/.
(2) /z/ after any other voiced sound.
(3) /s/ in all other cases.

These rules, however, apply only to *s* when it is one of the following morphemes:

(1) regular noun plural.
(2) third person singular, present indicative marker for the verb.
(3) singular or plural possessive marker.
(4) any of the contractions like *John's* (from *John is*).

The past tense marker *(e)d* functions similarly, but is not entirely regular. In all of these cases, nevertheless, the direct spelling-to-sound approach fails unless it is based upon morpheme identity — and if so, the approach is no longer a direct spelling-to-sound approach.

Another area in which the direct correspondence approach fails to recognize inherent patterning is in the treatment of the final clusters *gm* and *gn* which were mentioned above. Consider the forms *autumn: autumnal, damn: damnation, paradigm: paradigmatic, sign: signify*. It is not sufficient to state that *gn* and *gm* in final position correspond to /n/ and /m/, while in medial position to /-gn-/ and /-gm-/. Such rules fail in cases like *autumns, designing* and *signer*. There is no way to avoid reference to morphemes in this case, unless one simply enumerates the words for each pronunciation. A regular pattern is present in these forms, the most important aspect of which is the preservation of morpheme identity. The alternations of /g/ and zero in these examples, along with the alternations of the vowels preceding *g*, are predictable. The direct spelling-to-sound approach once again breaks down when morpheme identity becomes important.

b. *Form Class*

The school-book approach to orthography, as exemplified by *Webster's New Collegiate Dictionary*, recognizes *ng* as a spelling for /ŋ/ when this phoneme is not followed by /g/.

The digraph *ng*, as in *sing*, *singing*, represents the voiced tongue-back velar nasal continuant, corresponding to the voiced tongue-back stop *g*, and the voiceless tongue-back stop *k*.[6]

In contrast, the parallel cluster *mb* is analyzed phonotactically: "*b* is usually silent after *m* in the same syllable, as in *bomb*, *climb*, *thumb*, etc."[7] That *Webster's* treats identical phenomena in contrastive ways is only one of the problems here. Another problem is that an adequate description of the pronunciations of *ng* and *mb* must be based upon both morphemic and phonotactical relations. The pronunciation of any form ending in *nger* or *ngest* can not be predicted unless the morphemic identities of *er* and *est* are known. If these are the comparative and superlative markers, then *ng* is pronounced /ŋg/ as in *stronger*; in most other cases the /ŋg/ cluster is leveled to /ŋ/, just as it is in word final position. Morphemic identity is also important for predicting the pronunciation of word final *ate*. In adjectives and nouns, this ending is generally pronounced /-ɪt/, e.g., *duplicate*, *frigate*, *syndicate*, while in verbs, /-et/, e.g., *deflate*, *duplicate*, *integrate*.

A final example of where form class identity is necessary for correct pronunciation is in initial *th*. Functors beginning with this cluster have the voiced inter-dental spirant /ð/: *the*, *then*, *this*, *those*, while contentives have the voiceless spirant /θ/: *theses*, *thin*, *thumb*.[8]

4. PHONOTACTICAL INFLUENCES

a. *Consonant Clusters*

A knowledge of phoneme arrangements which are not allowed in English words is a necessary prerequisite for analyzing many spelling-to-sound correspondences. Sequences like /bp/ and /pb/ do not occur within English words — where they would occur, as in *subpoena* and *clapboard*, the speaker drops one sound or the

[6] *Webster's New Collegiate Dictionary*, 1953, p. xiv.
[7] *Ibid.*, p. xi.
[8] Functors and contentives are defined by Hockett, 1958, pp. 264ff.

other (with /pb/ and /bp/, the first sound is always omitted). While the spellings do not change, the pronunciations do. Yet, to label the pronunciation of *b* in *subpoena* as irregular, just as one does for the *b* in *debt*, is to ignore a pattern of English phonology. The elision of sounds in consonant clusters can be predicted, not only across morpheme boundaries, but also in initial and final positions, as in *knee*, *gnat*, *bomb*, and *sing*. In all of these cases, the correct pronunciation can be derived by first mapping all spelling units onto a pre-phonemic level and then applying the rules for leveling non-English clusters to obtain the phonemic forms. Thus, *knee*, *gnat*, *bomb*, *sing*, become first {kni}, {gnæt}, {bamb}, {sɪŋg}, and then the non-allowed clusters are leveled, giving /ni/, /næt/, /bam/, /sɪŋ/.

b. *Palatalization*

To predict consonant cluster leveling is not the only reason for observing the arrangements of phonemes in English words. The palatalization of /sj, zj, tj, dj/ to /š, ž, č, ǰ/ and the deletion of /j/ from the cluster /ju/ also depend upon this knowledge. In addition, many spelling-to-sound patterns which can be described only clumsily in direct spelling-to-sound terms are more adequately described in phonological terms. A preceding /w/, for example, tends to change /æ/ into /a/ when this vowel is not followed by a velar consonant, e.g., *swamp*, *assuage*, *quadrant*, *swan*, *quality*, *quantum*: *wag*, *quack*, *twang*, *wax*. To describe this process in direct spelling-to-sound terms is difficult. The various spellings which correspond to /w/ and to /k/, /g/, and /ŋ/ must be enumerated, and even if this is done, the phonological nature of the /æ/ → /a/ shift is not revealed.

5. DESCRIPTIVE MODEL

Whatever system of rules is chosen to relate spelling to sound must be not only accurate and as simple as possible, but also revealing, in the sense that it allows a differentiation of the various patterns in the system. To present the *x* patterns, which depend upon a graphemic distinction and stress placement, as parallel to the /w/ pattern discussed above is, as an example, an unsatisfactory account of the current orthography.

In the spelling-to-sound model employed here, graphemic words are divided into their graphemic allomorphs, and then these allomorphs are related to intermediate (morphophonemic) units by an ordered set of rules. Other rules then relate the morphophonemic units to phonemic forms. All rules which are based upon non-graphemic features are applied in an ordered sequence on the morphophonemic level, yielding various sub-levels of intermediate forms for each word. The final morphophonemic form is then mapped automatically onto the phonemic level. While the intermediate level is not strictly a morphophonemic level, it will be labeled as such hereafter. Its primary function is to separate graphemically dependent rules from grammatically and phonologically dependent ones.

As examples of how this model organizes spelling-to-sound rules, the processes for generating the pronunciations of *social* and *signing* are shown below:

social would be mapped into {sosɪæl} by the grapheme-to-morphophoneme rules for the separate units *s, o, c, i, a, l* (see Chapters V and VII). On the first morphophonemic level the main word stress would be placed on the first syllable, resulting in {sósɪæl}. Then through vowel reduction {-ɪæ-} would become {-jə-} and the resulting {-sj-} would be palatalized to {-š-}. The form {sóšəl} would then be mapped onto the phonemic level, giving /sóšəl/.
signing would first be broken into *sign* and *ing* and then each of these graphemic allomorphs would be mapped onto the morphophonemic level, yielding {sɪgn} and {ɪng}. Upon combination of the two forms and the application of stress and phonotactical rules, the form {sígnɪŋg} would result. By the rules for leveling consonant clusters, final {ŋg} would become {-ŋ} and {-gn-} would become {-n-} with compensatory alternation of {-ɪ-} to {aɪ-}. These operations yield {sáɪnɪŋ} which is automatically mapped into /saínɪŋ/.[9]

[9] A more detailed discussion of this model is given in Ruth H. Weir, *Formulation of Grapheme-Phoneme Correspondence Rules to Aid in the Teaching of Reading*, Cooperative Research Project S-039, Final Report (Stanford, 1964); Ruth H. Weir and Richard L. Venezky, *Rules to Aid in the Teaching of Reading*, Cooperative Research Project No. 2584, Final Report (Stanford, 1965).

IV

THE GRAPHEMIC SYSTEM

1. SELECTION OF UNITS

a. *The Grapheme-Phoneme Parallel*

The description of spelling-to-sound relationships begins with certain units on the spelling or graphic level and ends, for convenience, not with actual speech sounds, but with phonemes. Traditional studies in this area have generally employed the term grapheme as parallel to phoneme and various attempts have been made in recent years to formalize graphemics or to elaborate on the grapheme-phoneme parallel.[1]

> Borrowing some ideas and methods from phonemics and morphemics, for instance, we could conclude that each of the various letters has two or more different shapes, which seem to be in complementary distribution or free variation. This in turn suggests that each different shape can be called an *allograph*, and a family of allographs a *grapheme* ... Taking inventory of the segmental graphemes of standard English writing or printing, we find that there are thirty-seven of them, which can be classified in two groups:
> (a) Twenty-six letters of the alphabet ⟨abc ... z⟩
> (b) Eleven marks of punctuation ⟨, ; : . ? ! - " ( ) —⟩
> In addition we must include space, a sort of zero grapheme.[2]

[1] The earliest mention of the grapheme-phoneme parallel that I can find is in F. de Saussure, *Course in General Linguistics*, trans. Wade Baskin (New York, 1959), 23, 30. Saussure saw four features in the letters (he did not use the term GRAPHEME) which paralleled features in the phonemic system. Pulgram upped the count of parallel features to nine ("Phoneme and Grapheme: a Parallel", *Word*, 7 (1951), 15-20). For a summary of linguistic writings on the grapheme-phoneme parallel, see John C. McLaughlin, *A Graphemic-Phonemic Study of a Middle English Manuscript* (The Hague, 1963), 24-28.

[2] W. N. Francis, *Structure*, p. 436.

Even with this description, the graphemic and phonemic systems are far from parallel. While various single graphemes can be mapped (through intermediate levels) into single phonemes, there are also grapheme clusters that operate as single units, like *th* and *ch*. Since one cannot deduce the behavior of these clusters from the behavior of their constituents, it must be concluded that there exist units higher than the grapheme on the graphic level, like *ch* and *th*, which correspond more closely to the phoneme than does the grapheme. An adequate description of English graphics should, therefore, describe such units. To meet this need, Hall differentiates between simple and compound graphemes.

> The compound graphemes of English include a great many sequences of vowel letters, graphic diphthongs such as *ae*, *ai*, *au*, *ea*, *ei*, *eo*, ... *eu*, *ie*, *oa*, *oi*, *ou*, *ue*, in addition to double vowel letters like *ee* or *oo*. There are also certain combinations of consonant letters which function as single units and hence must be considered as compound graphemes: e.g., *ch*, *gh*, *ph*, *rh*, *sh*, *th*, *ng*, and again, all the double consonant letters such as *bb*, *dd*, etc.[3]

Even this division, however, does not create a workable parallel between grapheme and phoneme. Certain graphemes function solely as markers, that is, do not themselves enter into correspondences, but rather, mark one of several possible correspondences for other graphemes or grapheme clusters. Final *e*, for example, performs at least six different marking functions (see pages 55-58). It indicates vowel correspondences as in *mate* and *cute* (cf. *mat* and *cut*), it marks consonant correspondences as in *trace*, *change*, and *bathe* (cf. *bath*), and preserves graphotactical patterns as in *have*, *toe*, and *glue*. The phonemic level has no parallel to this.

One other major difference between graphemes and phonemes is that phonemes are language dependent, functionally-defined units, while graphemes are not necessarily language dependent nor functionally defined. Almost all speech communities which use the Roman alphabet have the same graphemic system, according to current definitions of graphemics, yet their phonemic sys-

[3] Robert A. Hall, Jr., *Sound and Spelling in English* (Philadelphia, 1961), 14.

tems are vastly different. Furthermore, a new grapheme can be added at will to the graphemic system, regardless of whether or not it contrasts functionally with existing graphemes. The Anglo-Norman scribes, for example, re-introduced *q* into English orthography. Yet this grapheme performed the same function as *k* which remained in the English writing system.[4] The parallel situation does not exist on the phonemic level; in fact, the opposite is true. A new phoneme comes into existence only when a new contrast appears.

The term 'grapheme' refers to letter classes. The individual letters, as written, typed, or in any other way produced, are called graphs, and each graph is classed under one of the twenty-six graphemes in the current alphabet. The decision to label two graphs as same or different depends in no way upon whether they function as the same or different form. Both *q* and *k*, for example, correspond only to /k/ (or are silent), yet *k* and *q* are not classed as members of the same grapheme. The difference between these two graphs, therefore, cannot depend upon the relationship of spelling to sound or upon any other language dependent feature, but only upon the graphic features of the two forms. This process of classification is vastly different from the process by which two phones are assigned to phonemes. Form alone is considered in classing graphs into grapheme patterns, but both form and function are essential for classing phones as members of phoneme classes.[5]

b. *Types of Graphemic Units*

In the remainder of this report GRAPHEME will refer to one of the

[4] Latin *q* occurred before *v* as a spelling for /kw/ in some early Old English manuscripts (see OED, *s.v. q*), but *cw* was a more common spelling for OE /kw/. After the Conquest *q* was re-introduced in English orthography by Anglo-Norman scribes and by the end of the thirteenth century *qu* had replaced *cw* and *kw* as a spelling for /kw/.

[5] The discrimination of graphemes has been studied by a number of psychologists in recent years and attempts have even been made to formulate distinctive features for letters. See especially Eleanor J. Gibson, *et al.*, "An Analysis of Critical Features of Letters, Tested by a Confusion Matrix", Harry Levin, ed. *A Basic Research Program on Reading* (Cornell, 1963).

alphabetic characters *a* through *z*, and the term GRAPHEMIC LEVEL will be used as a general reference for the spelling level.[6] The actual language-dependent units on the graphemic level which are significant for the prediction of sound are called FUNCTIONAL UNITS and are divided into two classes: RELATIONAL UNITS and MARKERS.

A RELATIONAL UNIT is a string of one or more graphemes which has a MORPHOPHONEMIC CORRESPONDENT which cannot be predicted from the behavior of the unit's smaller graphemic components.

A MARKER is a cluster of one or more graphemes whose primary function is to indicate the correspondences of relational units or to preserve a graphotactical or morphological pattern. It is mapped into a zero morphophoneme.

c. *Relational Units*

The same grapheme or grapheme cluster can be part of more than one relational unit. Thus, *gn* in *cognac* and *poignant* is a single relational unit which corresponds to the morphophonemic cluster {nj}, but *gn* in *sign* and *malign* is not a relational unit, but rather a combination of two relational units which correspond to the morphophonemes {g} and {n}. Morphophonemic rules map {g} into either {ø} or into {g}, depending upon allomorphic considerations (cf. *signal* and *malignant*). The selection of relational units is based upon function and composition. Any string of graphemes that corresponds to a non-zero morphophoneme is a potential relational unit. However, only those strings whose mor-

[6] GRAPHEME is not an ideal term, either, for the discussion of spelling-to-sound correspondences, but I find the only plausible substitute, LETTER, more objectionable. The case against LETTER was summarized by Angus McIntosh, "The Analysis of Written Middle English", *Trans. Phil. Soc.* (1956), p. 43. "The word 'letter' in everyday use is ambiguous. It may be employed in the sense of 'grapheme' as when we say that the word *swilk* begins with 'the letter *s*'; at other times it is used of the particular allographic form of a grapheme may have in a given context; e.g., when we speak of 'the *s* used in final position in Greek'; again, it may be used of a single instance of an allograph, as when we say 'that's a badly formed letter' ...."

phophonemic correspondences cannot be predicted by general rules based upon smaller units contained in the string are classed as relational units. *ch* in *chair*, for example, is a relational unit since the morphophoneme {č} cannot be predicted from general rules based upon *c* and *h* separately. Geminate consonant clusters, however, are not single relational units since their morphophonemic forms can be obtained from rules based upon their separate constituents. (The leveling of clusters like {ff} to {f} can be accounted for by a general phonotactical rule).

Consonant relational units, furthermore, are classed as functionally simple or functionally compound.[7] This distinction is needed for an accurate statement of a number of rules. In the sequence VOWEL + CONSONANT + FINAL *e*, for example, VOWEL is generally mapped into its free alternate if CONSONANT is a functionally simple unit (or this type of unit plus *l* or *r*), and into its checked alternate if CONSONANT is a functionally compound unit, or a cluster.[8] Thus,

Free alternate	*Checked alternate*
b*a*ke	*a*xe
*a*che	b*a*dge
conc*e*de	*e*dge
cl*o*the	h*o*dge

Vowel units are classed as primary (*a*, *e*, *i*, *y*, *o*, *u*), or secondary (all others).

Examples of markers are the final *e* in *mate* and *peace*, the *u* in *guest* and the *k* in *trafficking*, all of which indicate the pronunciation of a preceding grapheme. *ue* in *plague*, *catalogue*, etc., is a sequence of two markers. The *u* after *g* marks the correspondence *g* → {g} rather than *g* → {ǰ}. Since *u* generally does not appear in final position in English words (see page 62 for exceptions), a final *e* is added, as in *continue* and *blue* (cf. the alternations *ou*/*ow*, *au*/*aw*, pages 60-61). Only graphemes mapped into zero can

[7] The functionally compound units are *tch*, *dg*, *ck*, *wh*, and *x*. The remaining consonant units (including *sh*, *th*, and *ch*) are functionally simple.

[8] Free and checked vowels are described on page 14 and in Hans Kurath, *A Phonology and Prosody of Modern English* (Ann Arbor, 1964), 17-20.

be classed as markers (this is a necessary, but not sufficient condition). Graphemes with non-zero morphophonemic correspondences, however, though properly classed as relational units, can also perform marking functions. The *i* in *city*, for example, besides corresponding to {ɪ}, marks the correspondence *c* → {s}. A geminate consonant cluster also performs a marking function since it regularly indicates the correspondence of the preceding vowel.

The strongest evidence for a separate class of markers in English orthography is found in orthographic alternation patterns. For example, final *e* as a marker for the pronunciation of a preceding *c* or *g* is dropped before a suffix which begins with a letter that will perform the same function as the *e*. Therefore, *notice* drops the final *e* before *ing* (*noticing*) since *i* also marks the correspondence *c* → {s}, but retains the *e* before *able* since *noticable* would have *c* → {k}. Similarly, the *e* added to an otherwise terminal *u* is dropped before any suffix since the only function of the *e* is to avoid having word-final *u*, e.g., *argue*, *arguing*.

Relational units are classed as consonants or vowels depending upon the class of the morphophonemes into which they are mapped (glides are classed as consonants). Some RELATIONAL UNITS are classed as both consonants and vowels, e.g., *u* in *language* (consonant) and *during* (vowel). Within these classes major and minor patterns are distinguished on the basis of frequency of occurrence. Thus, *ch* is classed as a major consonant unit, but *kh* (*khaki*) is classed as a minor unit. While the major-minor classification may appear arbitrary, it distinguishes frequently occurring, productive patterns from infrequent patterns which generally occur in only a small number of borrowings.

In the traditional treatment of spelling, forms like *gu* (*guard*), *ti* (*nation*), *di* (*soldier*), and *a* ... *e* (*bake*) are adopted as basic spelling units.[9] Although such a course has not been adopted here, it is interesting and informative, nevertheless, to extend this treatment to some of its logical conclusions. In the units just mentioned, so-called silent letters are always included as parts of other spelling units, regardless of the functions which they per-

[9] See especially Hall, 1961, pp. 17-22.

form. Therefore, the *b* in *debt* and the final *e* in *peace* would fall into the same basket, in that they are both silent — the units, presumably, being *bt* and *ce*. This treatment, unfortunately, obscures a basic difference between these two silent letters, namely, that the *e* at the end of *peace* marks the correspondence *c* → {s} while the *b* in *debt* is a functionless scribal insertion. The *e* at the end of *peace* is part of the general pattern of markers in English orthography; the *b* in *debt*, on the other hand, is an unproductive, isolated occurrence.

Consider, furthermore, the traditional enumeration of spelling units as reflected in such words as *clothe* and *pace*. Both words have, by the traditional treatment, a silent *e* which must be attached to another grapheme, yet it is not clear which unit either *e* should be attached to, since in each word it marks two separate patterns. In *clothe e* marks the correspondences *o* → {o} and *th* → {ð}; in *pace* it marks *a* → {e} and *c* → {s}. The traditionalist is faced with a dilemma here; are the units *o* ... *e*/*a* ... *e* or *the*/*ce*? Or shall we take a fine razor and split *e* into two parts so that both alternatives can be taken? Without treating *e* as a member of a class of markers that are separate from the relational units, no realistic solution is possible.

The last of the major problems inherent in the traditional view is that an unnecessarily large number of basic units are created by the merger of markers with relational units. Besides classing all of the geminate consonant clusters as basic units, the following, among others, must also be recognized as basic:

the	breathe	ce	trace
dge	edge	lle	belle
le	able	gne	cologne
re	acre	ffe	giraffe
ye	bye	aoh	pharaoh
ge	change	ah	pariah
xe	axe	eh	vehement
ve	love		

All of the units above must be classed as basic units by the traditional view, yet their behavior can be predicted from the behavior of their components. The final *e* in the clusters shown above is a marker whose various functions are explained on pages 56-58. Geminate clusters (*belle*, *giraffe*) can be handled by considering each consonant separately and leveling the resulting geminate morphophonemic clusters by a single rule. *h* in *pharaoh* and *pariah* is a marker (see page 56), while in *vehement* it is deleted by a phonotactic rule (cf. *vehicle*; *vehicular*).

d. *Enumeration of Relation Units*

The consonant and vowel relational units are shown below. Units followed by an asterisk are discussed in the following paragraphs.

Major Relational Units

Consonants						Vowels			
simple					compound	primary	secondary		
b	gh	n	s	w*	ck*	a	ai/ay	ie	ue
c	h	p	sh	y*	dg	e	au/aw	oa	ui
ch	j	ph	t	z	tch	i	ea	oe	
d	k	q	th		wh	o	ee	oi/oy	
f	l	r	u*		x	u	ei/ey	oo	
g	m	rh	v			y	eu/ew	ou/ow	

Minor Relational Units

Consonants		Vowels
simple	compound	secondary
kh	gn	ae
sch		eau
		eo
		uy

u is a consonant unit when it corresponds to {w} as in *quack*, *language* and *assuage*. It may also be a vowel unit, or part of a vowel unit (*ou*), or a marker (*guest*, *plague*).

w is a consonant unit when it corresponds to {w}, e.g., *warm*, *beware*. It also appears as part of a vowel unit (*ow*, *aw*) but never as a vowel unit by itself.

y is a consonant unit when it corresponds to {j}, e.g., *yes, beyond.* It also appears as a vowel unit, and as part of a vowel unit, e.g., *cycle, boy.*

ck is a consonant unit in words like *rack* and *tack*. In instances like *picnicking*, however, the *k* is a marker. That *ck* in *picnicking* is identical to the relational unit *ck* is immaterial, since the base form *picnic* ends in *c*, not *ck*.

e. *Examples of Minor Units*

kh	khaki, khan	eau	bureau, plateau
sch	schist, schwa	eo	jeopardy, leopard
gn	cognac, poignant	uy	buy, guy
ae	aesthetic, algae		

2. MARKERS

a. *Introduction*

The primary functions of markers, as mentioned above, are to indicate the correspondences of other graphemes and to preserve graphotactical or morphological patterns. For example, *v* does not occur in final position in English; where it would, a final *e* has been added, e.g., *have*, *love*. Various relational units also serve as markers, but since they have non-zero morphophonemic correspondents, they are classed as relational units rather than as markers. In the discussion below, markers are classed according to the functions they perform.

b. *Markers of Vowel Correspondences*

(1) In the word-final patterns *VCe* and *VCle*, *e* generally indicates the free pronunciation of *V*.[10] Thus, *mate* : *mat*, *mete* : *met*, *site* : *sit*, *note* : *not*, *cute* : *cut*.

[10] See Weir, 1964, pp. 42-45.

(2) *h*. Post vocalic *h* before a consonant or juncture is classed as a marker, even though no clear marking function can be determined from the few existing occurrences of this form: *ah, hurrah, oh, pharaoh, pariah, hallelujah*.[11] (The alternative is to class *ah, oh*, and *aoh* as relational units). In *prohibition, vehement*, etc., *h* is mapped into {h} and then deleted by a general morphophonemic rule.

c. *Markers of Consonant Correspondences*

(1) *e*. In final position after *c*, *e* marks the correspondence *c* → {s}. In adding suffixes which do not begin with *i, y*, or *e*, the *e* is retained as a marker, e.g., *trace* : *traceable* : *tracing*.[12]

(2) *e*. In final position after *consonant* + *l* or *consonant* + *r*, *e* marks a syllabic *l* or *r*. Thus, *able, table, acre, massacre*. Consonant + *re* spellings are rare in American English, occurring regularly only in the patterns *cre* and *gre* where the more normal *cer* and *ger* would indicate the wrong pronunciations for *c* and *g*.

(3) *e*. In final position after *g*, *e* marks the correspondence *g* → {ǰ}, e.g., *age, college*. After *dg*, *e* is a graphotactical marker, since *dg* does not occur in final position. In adding suffixes which do not begin with the *i, y*, or *e*, the *e* is retained as a marker, e.g., *change* : *changeable* : *changing*. In final position after *th*, *e* marks the correspondence *th* → {ð}. Thus, *bath* : *bathe*, *breath* : *breathe*, *teeth* : *teethe*, *cloth* : *clothe*, *wreath* : *wreathe*.

(4) *u*. After *g*, *u* is occasionally used to mark the correspondence *g* → {g} (cf. the use of *e* to mark *g* → {ǰ}, above). For example, *guess, guide, guest, guise, catalogue, guilt, plague, guild*.

(5) *k*. A *k* is inserted between a final *c* and a suffix beginning with *i, y*, or *e*, to mark the correspondence *c* → {k}. Thus, *picnic* : *picnicking*, *traffic* : *trafficking*, *panic* : *panicky*, *shellac* : *shellacked*.[13]

[11] *Ohm* and other German borrowings are not considered here.

[12] *e* simultaneously performs two marking functions in *trace*; it marks the correspondences *a* → {e} and *c* → {s}.

[13] But, irregularly, *arc:arcing, disc:discing:disced*. Note, however, the tendency to respell *disc* as *disk*. In *lyricism* (cf. *lyric, lyrical*) the phonetic change in Latin of [k] → [s] obviated the need for the *k* marker.

(6) GEMINATION. A geminate consonant cluster regularly marks a checked correspondent for a preceding vowel. Compare, for example, *anal* : *annals*, *fetal* : *fetter*, *hypo* : *hippo*, *rotor* : *rotter* (*blackguard*), *super* : *supper*.

d. *Markers of Graphotactical Patterns*

(1) *e*. After what would otherwise be a final *v* or *u*, an *e* is added. This practice developed during the late Middle English period, due partially to the graphical identity of *u* and *v*. Thus, *love*, *glue*, *have*, *plague*, *glove*, *continue*.

(2) *e*. To limit the two-letter words in English to a select group of common words, a final *e* has been added after a vowel in what would otherwise have been a two-letter word. Thus, *see*, *doe*, *toe*, *rye*, etc. On the addition of *e* after *o*, Webster's 1852 *Dictionary* had the following explanation:

> Woe. — This word takes the final *e*, like *doe*, *foe*, *hoe*, *sloe*, *toe*, and all similar nouns of one syllable. The termination in *o* belongs among monosyllables, to the other parts of speech, as *potato*, *tomato*, etc.[14]

(3) *al*. The cluster *al* is inserted between a final adjectival *ic* and the adverbial *ly* if an adjective in *ical* does not exist. Thus, *basic* : *basically*, *rustic* : *rustically*, *scenic* : *scenically*. Generally, the *al* is mapped into zero in such forms. Spelling pronunciations, however, have introduced forms in which the *al* is pronounced.

e. *Markers of Morphemic Patterns*

After a number of words which would otherwise end in non-morphemic *s*, an *e* has been added to avoid the appearance of a final, inflectional *s*. Thus, *moose*, *goose*, *mouse*. After the cluster *rs*, *e* also marks the correspondence *s* → {s} in contrast to *s* → {z}

[14] *Webster's American Dictionary of the English Language*, ed. Chauncey A. Goodrich (2d ed. rev.; Springfield, Mass., 1852), p. 81. Two-letter words ending in a consonant were lengthened, not by adding a final *e*, but rather, by doubling the final consonant; thus, *ebb*, *add*, *odd*, *egg*, *inn*. (These are the only examples of final *bb*, *dd*, *gg*, *nn* in Modern English spelling).

(cf. *hearse* : *hers*). Non-morphemic *s* is generally avoided in final position in nouns, adjectives (by analogy to nouns), and verbs under the following conditions:

(a) when preceded by a consonant

collapse	dense
eclipse	sense
else	hearse
false	coarse

(b) when preceded by a compound vowel

goose	praise
moose	raise
house	noise
mouse	poise

The only true exceptions to these restrictions are *summons* (n., sg.), *lens*, and words ending in *ous*. *Summons*, an Anglo-French adoption, had variant spellings in *nce* and *nse* through the seventeenth century (see OED, *s.v.*), but apparently through analogy (both spelling and pronunciation) with the identical form, *summons* became the standard spelling. *Lens* is a late seventeenth century Latin adoption for which no variant spellings in *se* were found in the data used for this study. If, however, this word were a phonological rather than a spelling adoption, then *lense* would give the incorrect pronunciation /lɛns/. (This is also true of *summonse*). The suffix *ous*, if spelled *ouse* would be pronounced /*aus*/ as in *mouse* and *house*. Apparent exceptions to (1) and (2) above are words like *hydraulics*, *mathematics*, *mumps*, and *billiards*, which function as both singulars and plurals. In these, however, the *s* can be classed as a morphemic unit.

The only situations where the *e* marker is not added is where *s* is preceded by a simple vowel spelling, but here *e* cannot be added because it would tend to mark an incorrect pronunciation for the simple vowels. Compare *us* : *use*, *his* : *rise*, *locus* : *recluse*, *tennis* : *improvise*.

3. GRAPHEMIC ALTERNATIONS

a. *i* and *y*

Vocalic *i* and *y* (which can be considered as members of the same functional unit) occur in complementary distribution: *y* in final position and *i* in initial and medial position. There are, however, numerous exceptions to this pattern. A considerable number of Greek and Latin borrowings retain *y* in medial position, e.g., *embryo, asylum, rhythm*. In addition, some medial *y*'s have resulted from inorganic final *e*'s, e.g., *rye* and *bye*, and from scribal pedantry, as in *rhyme* which was converted from the earlier *rime* on the mistaken analogy with L. *rhythm*. Initial *y* (vowel) occurs in the forms *ycleped*, *yttrium*, and *ytterbium*, while final *i* occurs in several distinct patterns. One is the plural of Latin borrowings whose singulars end in *-us*, e.g., *alumni*, *fungi*, *magi*, and *stimuli* (*alibi* and *quasi* are singular in Latin). Similarly, it occurs as the plural of Italian borrowings whose singulars (used in Italian only) end in *o*, e.g., *broccoli* (It. sg. *broccolo*), *confetti* (It. sg. *confetto*), *ravioli* (It. sg. *raviolo*), and *spaghetti* (It. sg. *spaghetto*). *Macaroni*, another Italian borrowing, is singular in Italian. Of the remaining words ending in *i*, *alkali*, *charivari*, *houri*, and *potpourri* are French, *anti* is Greek, *ski* is Norwegian, *chilli* is Mexican, *khaki* is Urdu, *mufti* is Arabic, *yogi* is Hindustani, and *taxi* is an early twentieth century American coining. Many of these words had alternate final spellings in *y* or *ee*, but apparently a desire to retain the foreign appearance favored the final *i* spellings.

The alternation of *i* and *y* occurs with suffixation in the following cases (for exceptions, see *Webster's New Collegiate Dictionary*, 1956, pp. 1145-47):

(1) When *ing* is added to words ending in *ie*, *e* is dropped and *i* is changed to *y*, e.g., *die* : *dying*, *tie* : *tying*.
(2) When a suffix not beginning with *i* is added to a base ending in *y*, *y* changes to *i*, e.g., *icy* : *iciest*, *mercy* : *merciless*.
(3) A few words which end in *vowel* + *y* irregularly change *y* to *i* before some suffixes, e.g., *day* : *daily*, *lay* : *laid*.

i and *y* also alternate as parts of the compound vowel units *ai* (*ay*) *ei* (*ey*), and *oi* (*oy*), the *y* alternate appearing before vowels and word juncture and the *i* alternate appearing in all other cases. Exceptions to this pattern are the following:

geyser An Icelandic borrowing, taken from the name of a hot spring in Iceland.

moiety A ME adoption of OF *moite*, *moitie.* The earlier form *moitie* was replaced by *moiety* in the last half of the seventeenth century. The middle vowel in the pronunciation is probably excrescent.

oyster A ME adoption of OF *oistre*, *uistre.* Judging from the OED entries for this word, *oy* was the only spelling commonly employed.

paranoia A late nineteenth century Latin adoption. The *oia* spelling was probably retained because of its similiarity to other medical terms ending in *ia*, e.g., *megalomania*, *malaria*, *anemia*, *dementia* and *hysteria.*

sequoia A Latinization (in botanical terms generally) from *Sequoiah*, a Cherokee Indian name.

b. *u* and *w*

As consonant spellings, *u* and *w* are, for the most part, in complementary distribution. *u* appears as a spelling for *w* in the environments *gu*, *su*, *qu* (initial and medial), *ju*, *nu* (all medial) *pu* and *cu* (initial). *w* occurs in all other cases, except for the three forms *suave*, *suede*, and *suite.* Following is an exhaustive listing of occurrences of these spellings in the corpus used for this study.

gu	*su*	*ju*
anguish	assuage	marijuana
distinguish	persuade	
extinguish	*pu*	*nu*
jaguar	pueblo	ennui
language		
languid		

	cu
lingual	cuisine
linguist	
penguin	
sanguine	
unguent	

u and *w* also alternate as the second parts of the compound vowel spellings which begin with *a*, *e*, and *o*. The *w* variant generally appears before another vowel spelling and in morpheme final positions, while the *u* variant occurs in all other positions. This pattern, however, is far from regular.

c. *Examples of Regular Spellings*

au	*aw*	*eu*	*ew*	*ou*	*ow*
auction	awe	eucharist	ewe	ounce	coward
audit	draw	eulogy	ewer	oust	however
augur	gnaw	feud	brewer	out	power
applaud	saw	neuter	shrewe	compound	allow
fault	straw	pneumatic	flew	south	cow
trauma	thaw	rheumatism	threw	trousers	vow

d. *Exceptions*

(a) *aw* in initial and medial position before a consonant

awkward	dawn
awl	scrawl
awning	spawn

(b) *ew* in medial position before a consonant

newt	lewd
pewter	shrewd

(c) *ou* in final position

bayou	bijou
caribou	thou
you	

(d) *ow* in initial and medial position before a consonant

owl	drowse
own	fowl
crowd	town

u in final position in English orthography is rare. Besides the examples given above, the only other examples are the following:

beau	adieu	flu
bureau	lieu	gnu
chateau		impromptu
plateau		menu
portmanteau		parvenu
trousseau		tabu
		virtu

e. *ous* and *ou*

The suffix *ous* becomes *os* before *ity*. Thus, *viscous* : *viscosity*, *curious* : *curiosity*, *generous* : *generosity*, *porous* : *porosity*, *monstrous* : *monstrosity*.

f. *i* and *e*

In the suffix *ity*, *i* becomes *e* when preceded by *i*. Thus *society* : *propriety*, *piety* : *satiety*, *contrariety* : *anxiety*, *variety* : *sobriety*.

V

CONSONANT DISTRIBUTIONS, CORRESPONDENCES, AND ALTERNATIONS

1. INTRODUCTION

The descriptions which follow of the consonant units include brief discussions of these topics:

DISTRIBUTION. The intra-word positions the unit commonly occupies, both by itself (i.e., contiguous with vowels or word boundaries only) and in combination with other consonant units (i.e., in consonant clusters).[1] Since only monomorphemic clusters are considered, such clusters as *-xts* as in *texts* are not included in this discussion.

CORRESPONDENCES. The spelling-to-morphophoneme correspondences for the consonant unit, presented as a set of ordered rules.

ALTERNATIONS. The productive morphophonemic and phonotactical alternations which are based upon the particular consonant unit, presented as a set of ordered rules. Non-productive alternations are listed with examples, but are not included in the ordered rules.[2]

[1] Since spelling units rather than letters of the alphabet form the basis of this discussion, the term cluster could be ambiguous. *tch*, for example, is a single spelling unit, yet is classed as a cluster in most treatments of the orthography. In this paper cluster will refer to a sequence of functional units only. The statement that a particular spelling unit appears in certain positions in a word (initial, medial, final) precludes occurrences of that unit in clusters. Clusters are always treated separately and, except for rare examples, only initial and final clusters which occur wholly within single morphemes are discussed. (With a broad enough definition of WORD, any cluster could occur in medial position).

[2] The classes PRODUCTIVE and NON-PRODUCTIVE are used here to separate patterns which we would tend to include in a description of the morphophon-

2. THE CORRESPONDENCES

b

a. *Distribution*

Initial and medial *b* account for almost 95 percent of all occurrences of this unit; final *b* is rare and final *bb* is rarer, occurring only in *ebb*, derived from OE *ebba*. In initial and final clusters *b* occurs chiefly with *r* and *l*, forming the initial clusters, *br-* and *bl-* and the final clusters, *-rb* and *-lb*, e.g., *brake*, *black*, *herb*, *curb*, *bulb*. Final *-lb* occurs only in *bulb* while final *-rb* occurs in about fifteen different words.[3] Two other final clusters, *-bt* and *-mb* occur, although they represent different patterns from the *-rb* and *-lb* clusters (see below).

b. *Correspondences*

(1) *b* in *debt*, *doubt*, and *subtle* corresponds to {ø}.[4]
(2) *b* elsewhere corresponds to {b}.

c. *Alternations*

(1) Initial {b} in {bd-} and morpheme final {b} in {-mb} are

emics and phonotactics of English from those we would not. In certain cases this classification is obvious, in others, quite arbitrary. The palatalization of {tj} to {č}, for example, is an active process in Modern English and therefore is a productive pattern; the alternation of {b} with zero in *number:numeric* is an isolated pattern, resulting from borrowing the same word from two different languages (Latin and French). But whether the alternation of {ɪ} and {ai} in *sign:signal* is productive or non-productive is difficult to determine (it is classed as non-productive here).

[3] Unless otherwise qualified, WORD implies the base form only and not the derivational and inflectional forms derived from the base. The separation of base forms from derived forms is not discussed in this paper. For a recent discussion on this topic, see Hans Marchand, *The Categories and Types of Present-Day English Word-Formation* (Wiesbaden, 1960).

[4] There is a variant pronunciation of *subtile* which has no /b/. This could lead to a {b}—{ø} alternation between *subtile* ({sə́təl}) and *subtility* ({səb-tɪlɪtɪ}).

dropped.[5] (*Bombard* is classed as a non-productive alternation with *bomb*; see below).

(2) In the medial combination *bilabial stop* + *bilabial stop*, the first stop is dropped. Cf., for example, *cupboard, subpoena, clapboard, raspberry.*

(3) Non-productive alternations:

{b} — {ø}	
bombard	bomb
crumble	crumb
debit	debt
iambic	iamb
indubitable	doubt
number	numeric
rhombus	rhomb
thimble	thumb

c

a. *Distribution*

c occurs primarily in initial and medial position; in final position it occurs in the ending *-ic* and in the borrowings *arc, havoc, sac, shellac, sumac, talc,* and *zodiac.* The low frequency of final *c* is probably due to the problems created by derivational and inflectional suffixes which begin with the vowels *e, i, y.* In such cases, *c* would be pronounced /s/ unless a *k* were added between *c* and the first vowel of the suffix. This is generally what is done after *-ic,* cf. *traffic* : *trafficking, picnic* : *picnicked,* but, irregularly, *arc* : *arcing.* In *lyric* : *lyricism* /k/ changes to /s/ so the spelling does not have to be altered. *c* also occurs in the initial clusters *cl-* (*clean, clover*), *cr-* (*crawl, crust*), *cz-* (*czar*), and *scr-* (*scream, screw*), and in the final cluster *-ct* (*abduct, sect*).

[5] Hypercorrect pronunciations of *iamb* and *rhomb* have a final (-mb) cluster.

b. *Correspondences*

(1) *c* in *cello* and *concerto* corresponds to {č}.
(2) *c* in *victual*, *czar*, and *indict* corresponds to {ø}.
(3) *c* before the spellings *i*, *y*, *e* (and in *facade*) corresponds to {s} (except in *sceptic*, an alternate spelling of *skeptic*, where it corresponds to {k}).
(4) *c* in all other positions corresponds to {k}.

c. *Alternations*

(1) {sj} before an unstressed vowel and in *sure* and *sugar* corresponds to {š}.[6]
(2) Non-productive alternations

{k} — {ø}

corpuscular	corpuscle
muscular	muscle

{k} — {s}

lyric	lyricism
music	musician

ch

a. *Distribution*

ch occurs frequently in initial and medial position and not so frequently in final position. It rarely occurs in clusters, the most common being *chl-*, *chr-*, and *-rch*, e.g., *chlorine*, *chrome*, *arch*. Much rarer are *-cht* and *-chm*, e.g., *yacht*, *drachm*.

b. *Correspondences*

(1) *ch* in *fuchsia*, *yacht*, and *drachm* corresponds to {ø}.

[6] This process (palatalization) is discussed in Chapter VI.

(2) *ch* corresponds to {k} before *l*, *n*, *r*, and in the following (plus their derivatives):

ache
alchemy
anarchy
anchor
archaeology
archaic
archangel
archetype
architect
architecture
archive
catechism
chameleon
chaos
character
chasm
chemi-
chiropodist
choir
choler
cholera
choral
chord
chorus
dichotomy
echo
epoch
eucharist
eunuch
hierarchy
hypochondria
lichen
machination
mechanic
melancholy
monarchy
orchestra
orchid
parochial
patriarch
pentateuch
psych-
stomach

(3) *ch* corresponds to {š} in the following words:

cache
chagrin
chaise
chalet
challis
chamois
champagne
chandelier
chanty
chaperon
charade
charivari
charlatan
chassis
chateau
chauffeur
chauvinism
chef
chemise
cheroot
chevalier
chevior
chevron
chic
chicanery
chiffon
chivalry
chute
cliche
crochet
echelon
machine
mustache
parachute
ricochet
sachet
stanchion

(4) In all other cases, *ch* corresponds to {č}.

c. *Alternations*

None. (On {k} — {č}, see *Alternations* under *k*).

d

a. *Distributions*

d occurs commonly in initial, medial, and final position and in the clusters *dr-* : *draw, dregs*; *dw-* : *dwell, dwindle*; *-nd* : *land, find*; *-ld* : *weld, bold*; *-rd* : *beard, board.* It also occurs in the cluster *-dz* in *adz.*

b. *Correspondences*

d regularly corresponds to {d}. (The identity of the past tense and participle marker {d} must be retained at the morphophonemic level so that the alternation of {d} and {t} can be handled correctly).

c. *Alternations*

(1) After all unvoiced final consonants except {t} the past tense and participle marker {d} becomes {t}.[7]

(2) {d} corresponds to {ø} between {n} and another consonant, as in *handkerchief.* Modern pronunciation is too unsettled, however, for the application of this rule to be more definitely delimited. It applies generally to *hands, pounds, stands, handful, grandmother*, but less frequently to *handstroke*, and *landslide* (see Gimson, p. 232).

[7] For a list of exceptions to this rule, see Albert H. Marckwardt, "Origin and extension of the voiceless preterit and the past participle inflections of the English irregular weak verb conjugation", University of Michigan Publications: *Essays and Studies in English and Comparative Literature*, Vol. XII, pp. 151-328 (Ann Arbor, 1935).

(3) {dj} palatalizes to {ǰ} before unstressed {u}.
(4) Non-productive alternations.

{d} — {s}

defend	defense
expend	expense
respond	response

{d} — {ø}

sound	sonant
spindle	spin

f

a. *Distribution*

f, which alternates in some environments with *ph*, occurs in initial, medial and final position. It also occurs in the following common clusters: *fl-*, *fr-*, *-lf*, *-rf*, *-ft*, e.g., *flood*, *free*, *half*, *serf*, *raft*.

b. *Correspondences*

(1) *f* in *of* corresponds to {v}.
(2) In all other cases, *f* corresponds to {f}.

c. *Alternations*

See also Chapter VI.

(1) In the following words morpheme final {f} becomes {v} with the addition of the regular plural morpheme: *calf*, *elf*, *half*, *knife*, *leaf*, *life*, *loaf*, *self*, *sheaf*, *shelf*, *staff*, *thief*, *wife*, *wolf*.
(2) In the following words, morpheme-final {f} becomes {v} when the noun becomes a verb:[8] (cf. *house* (n): *house* (v), *breath* : *breathe*).

[8] There is, however, an equally long list of words in which final {f} in the noun does not alternate with a final {v} in the verb: *brief*, *dwarf*, *leaf*, *sniff*, *spoof*, *stuff*, *whiff*.

belief	believe
grief	grieve
half	halve
life	live
proof	prove
relief	relieve
shelf	shelve
thief	thieve

(3) {f} in all other cases remains {f}.

(4) Non-productive alternations:

{f} — {v}

bereft	bereave
cleft	cleave
drift	drive
fifth	five
gift	give
left	leave
serf	serve
twelfth	twelve

g

a. *Distribution*

g occurs predominantly in initial and medial position in Modern English words. A small number of words, almost all monosyllables, have final *g*, e.g., *bag*, *bug*, *frog*, *hog*, *twig*. *g* also occurs in the initial clusters *gl-*, *gn*, *gr-*, e.g., *glide*, *gnat*, *grow*, and in the final clusters *-gm* and *-gn*, e.g., *paradigm*, *sign*. (Because of its highly irregular correspondences, *gg* is treated separately).

b. *Correspondences*

(1) *g* corresponds to {ø} in *seraglio*, *intaglio*, and *imbroglio*.

(2) *g* corresponds to {ž} in the following words (some of which have alternate pronunciations {ǰ}):

bourgeois	mirage
camouflage	prestige
corsage	protégé
garage	regime
lingerie	rouge
loge	sabotage
massage	

(3) *g* in *gaol* and *margarine* corresponds to {ǰ}.

(4) *g* corresponds to {g} before *e*, *i*, *y* in the following:

anger	geyser	girth
auger	giddy	give
begin	gift	gizzard
bogey	gig	gynaecology
conger	giggle	hunger
eager	gild	lager
finger	gilt	linger
fogey	gill	malinger
fungi	gimlet	monger
gear	gird	target
geese	girt	tiger
geld	girdle	yogi
get	girl	

(5) *g* before *e*, *i*, and *y* corresponds to {ǰ}.

(6) *g* otherwise corresponds to {g}.[9]

c. *Alternations*

(1) Morpheme final {-ŋg} becomes {ŋ} except before the comparative and superlative morphemes, where it remains as {-ŋg}. Thus {strəŋ} : {strɔ́ŋgər}, but {saɪn} : {saɪ́nər}.[10]

(2) Word initial {gn-} becomes {n} (cf. *gnostic* and *agnostic*).

[9] For other exceptions to rules 4 and 5, see Weir, 1964, p. 35.

[10] Besides *strong*, the only other eligible forms are *long*, *wrong*, and *young*. However, some suffixed forms of *long* and *diphthong*, retain {ŋg} — *elongate*, *elongation*, *diphthongize*, *prolongate*, *prolongation*. Note also *ting: tingle*.

(3) Morpheme final {-gn} and {-gm} become {n} and {m}. Thus, *sign* : {saɪn}, but *signal* : {sɪgnal}, *paradigm* : {pǽrədaɪm}, but *paradigmatic* : {pærədɪgmǽtɪk}.
(4) {g} in all other cases corresponds to {g}.

gg

a. *Distribution*

gg has a limited distribution in English words. It occurs in final position in one word: *egg*. In medial position it occurs predominately before final *-y* or *-er*, e.g., *baggy*, *dagger*. It occurs before *a* in the endings *-ar* (e.g., *beggar*), *-art* (e.g., *braggart*), and *-ard* (e.g., *loggard*), and in *baggage*, *luggage* and *toboggan. Maggot* is the only example found with *gg* before *o*. In addition, *gg* occurs in the medial clusters *ggl* and *ggr*, e.g., *giggle*, *aggrandize*.

b. *Correspondences*

(1) *gg* in *exaggerate* corresponds to {ǰ}.
(2) *gg* in *suggest* corresponds to {gǰ}.
(3) *gg* otherwise corresponds to {gg}.

c. *Alternations*

None.

gh

a. *Distribution*

gh is uncommon in English orthography, occurring mostly in initial and final position and in the cluster *-ght*, as in *night*, *might*, *nought* and *fought*.

b. *Correspondences*

(1) *gh* in *hough* corresponds to {k}.
(2) *gh* corresponds to {f} in the following:

clough	rough
cough	slough
draught	sough
enough	tough
laugh(ter)	trough

(3) Initial *gh* corresponds regularly to {g}, e.g., *ghastly*, *gherkin*, *ghetto*, *ghost* and *ghoul*.
(4) *gh* corresponds to {g} in the following words.

aghast	sorghum
burgh(er)	spaghetti[11]
dinghy	

(5) In all other cases, *gh* corresponds to {ø}.

c. *Alternations*

None.

h

a. *Distribution*

The consonant spelling *h* occurs in both initial and medial positions; in some medial positions and in all final positions it occurs only as a marker after a vowel. "It is intended to suggest stressed free vowels, as in the exclamations ah!, oh!, hurrah!, bah!, and in shah and Yahweh".[12] The OED suggests that besides marking a

[11] In *gherkin*, *ghetto*, *burgher*, *dinghy*, and *spaghetti*, *h* could be treated as a marker for g → {g}. *Gherkin*, *burgher*, and *dinghy* have earlier spellings without *h* (*gerkin*, *burger*, *dingy*); *ghetto* and *spaghetti* were borrowed from Italian where the *gh* spelling was common. (In *ghost* and *ghoul*, an earlier *g* spelling was changed in the sixteenth century to *gh*, apparently through the influence of Caxton).

[12] Kurath, 1965, p. 67.

'long' (free) vowel, *h* also marks non-native words. "After a vowel *h* is regularly silent, and such a vowel being usually long. ... the addition of *h* ... is one of the expedients which we have for indicating a long vowel in foreign or dialect words.[13]

b. *Correspondences*

(1) Initial *h* in *heir, herb, honest, honor, hour* corresponds to {ø}.
(2) Medial *h* before a consonant, and final *h* are markers for the preceding vowel and therefore correspond to {ø}, e.g., *fahrenheit, hurrah, pharaoh.*
(3) *h* in all other positions corresponds to {h}, e.g., *exhale, harmonic, vehicle.*

c. *Alternations*

(1) {h} preceded by a consonant corresponds to {ø} in most English dialects, cf., e.g., *philharmonic* : *harmonic.*
(2) Intervocalic {h}, when preceded by a stressed vowel, corresponds to {ø}, cf., e.g., *vehicle* : *vehicular.*
(3) In all other cases {h} corresponds to {h}.

j

a. *Distribution*

The letter *j* appears primarily in initial positions before back vowel spellings, but occasionally in medial position before either back or front vowel spellings, as in *cajole, deject, majesty, rajah.* In a number of cases where *j* appears before a front-vowel spelling, a variant spelling with *g* exists, e.g., *jest* : *gest*; *jingle* : *gingle*; *serjeant*:*sergeant* (now differentiated in meaning). The Hebrew loan word *hallelujah* has the variant (*h*)*alleluia*, while the American-

[13] OED, *s.v. h.*

Spanish *marijuana* has the variant *marihuana*. *j* does not appear in final position or in consonant clusters.

b. *Correspondences*

j regularly corresponds to {ǰ}, except in *bijou* ({ž}), *hallelujah*, ({j}), and *marijuana* ({ø}).

c. *Alternations*

None.

k

a. *Distribution*

k occurs in initial, medial and final position, but is limited to certain environments in each of these positions. In initial position it appears most commonly before *e* and *i* (both alone and in the cluster *sk-*) and in the cluster *kn-*. It does occur, however, in several recent borrowings before *a*, *o*, and *u*, e.g., *kaffir*, *kangaroo*, *kosher*, *kulak*. In final position it appears commonly after the vowel spellings *ea*, *ee*, *oa*, and *oo* as in *seek*, *soak*, and *took*, and in the clusters *-lk*, *-nk*, *-rk* and *-sk*, e.g., *milk*, *rank*, *hark*, and *ask*. Since *kk* is avoided in English orthography, *k* rarely occurs in final position after a stressed, single-letter vowel spelling, because in such positions it would double before suffixes which begin with a vowel. (The only common exception is *trek* — a mid-nineteenth century borrowing from African Dutch). (On the spelling *ck*, see page 90). In medial position it occurs chiefly before *e* and *i*. In words like *snake* and *dike* where the final *e* marks the correspondence of the preceding vowel, a *c* spelling for /k/ could not be used because the final *e* would also mark the incorrect correspondence for *c*.

b. *Correspondences*

k regularly corresponds to {k}.

c. *Alternations*

(1) Word initial {*kn-*} becomes {n}, as in *knee*, and *knowledge*. NOTE. In *acknowledge*, the {kn-} cluster is retained. This, however, is the only example of the retention of ME {kn-}. For the parallel retention of {gn-} (*agnostic:gnostic*), see *Alternations* under *g*.

(2) {k} in all other cases corresponds to {k}.

(3) Non-productive alternations.

{k} — {č}

speak	speech
leak	leach
wreak	wretch

l

a. *Distribution*

l occurs in initial, medial, and final position, as in *lamb*, *oleander*, and *coal*, and in a large number of monomorphemic clusters, the most common of which are shown below.

Initial clusters		*Final clusters*	
pl-	play	-lp	pulp
bl-	black	-lt	malt
cl-	climb	-ld	hold
chl-	chlorine	-lk	bulk
gl-	glaze	-lf	half
fl-	flower	-lch	belch
sl-	slip	-lm	helm
spl-	splash	-rl	curl
		-rld	world

Less common clusters are *-lb* : *bulb*, *-ltz* : *waltz*, *-lct* : *mulct*, and *-lx* : *calx*. Except in combinations with *r*, *l* always occurs next to a vowel in a consonant cluster.

b. *Correspondences*

(1) The first *l* in *colonel* corresponds to {r}.
(2) In *would*, *could* and *should*, *l* corresponds to {ø}.
(3) In all other cases *l* corresponds to {l}.

c. *Alternations*

(1) In morpheme-final {æ/a} + {l} + {k/m/v/f}, {l} corresponds to {ø}, e.g., *half*, *calm*, *chalk*, *halves*.
(2) In prejunctural position, consonant + {l} corresponds to consonant + {əl} (syllabic *l*), e.g., *simple* (cf. *simply*).
(3) In all other cases, {l} corresponds to {l}.

m

a. *Distribution*

m occurs commonly in initial, medial, and final position: *man*, *moon*, *demon*, *stamen*, *them*, *bloom*. It also occurs in the initial cluster *sm-*, e.g., *small*, *smooth*, and in the following monomorphemic final clusters:

-mp	limp, hemp
-mph	lymph, nymph
-lm	elm, helm
-rm	storm, arm
-sm	spasm, chasm
-thm	rhythm

b. *Correspondences*

(1) In *accompt* and *comptroller*, *m* corresponds to {n}.
(2) In all other cases, *m* corresponds to {m}.

c. *Alternations*

(1) The initial cluster {mn-} (*mnemonic*) is leveled to {n-}.
(2) After {ð} and {z}, pre-junctural {m} becomes {-əm} (syllabic *m*), e.g., *rhythm, spasm, schism.*
(3) Non-productive alternations.
  (a) *com-*, *con-*, *co-*, representing Latin *cum* 'with', 'together', 'very', e.g., *complex* (cf. *duplex*), *conclude* (cf. *include*), *coeval* (cf. *medieval*).
  (b) *sym-*, *syn-*, *syl-*, representing Greek *syn-* 'with', 'along with', 'at the same time', e.g., *symphonic*, (cf. *phonic*), *synonym*, (cf. *homonym*), *syllogism*, (cf. *antilogism*).

n

a. *Distribution*

n occurs in initial, medial, and final position, although more frequently in medial and final than in initial position. Besides the cluster *sn-* (*snow, snarl*), *n* also appears in the initial clusters *kn-* and *gn-*. In final position it appears in the following monomorphemic clusters:

-nch	pinch, wrench
-nd	and, bend
-nk	bank, drink
-nt	ant, infant
-nth	labyrinth
-gn	sign, malign
-ln	kiln
-rn	churn, concern

b. *Correspondences*

(1) *n* in *kiln* corresponds to {ø}.
(2) In all other cases *n* corresponds to {n}.

c. *Alternations*

(1) {n} before {k} and {g} becomes {ŋ} except in the stressed prefix-morphemes *con-*, *syn-*, and *in-*, and in the unstressed *un-*, where it remains as {n}.[14]
(2) {n} in all other cases corresponds to {n}.
(3) Non-productive alternations.

{n}	— {ø}
passenger	passage
messenger	message

p

a. *Distribution*

p occurs in initial, medial and final position by itself, and in a variety of clusters, the most common of which are *pr-*, *pl-*, *sp-*, *-lp*, *-rp*, *-sp*, e.g., *program*, *plough*, *speed*, *help*, *harp*, *asp*. A less common group of clusters which pattern quite differently from the ones above are *pn-* : *pneumonia*, *ps-* : *psychology*, *pt-* : *ptomaine*, *-pt* : *receipt*, *-rsp* : *corps*. The rules for handling these latter clusters are described below.

b. *Correspondences*

(1) *p* in *corps*, *coup*, and *receipt* corresponds to {ø}.

[14] This should not be taken as a rule, but as a compromise in a phonetically unstable situation. Kurath summarizes current practice as follows: "The prefixes *con-*, *in-*, *syn-*, when stressed have /n/ beside /ŋ/ before a following /k/... Before /g/, the velar /ŋ/ is fully established in *congress*, *congregate*, *ingot*, and fairly so in *congruence*, *congruous*. Occasionally /ŋ/ appears also in unstressed *con-*, *in-*, *syn-*, as in *conclude*, *concrete*, *include*, *increase*, *synchronic*." (Kurath, 1964, p. 71). To state the correspondence of *n* directly to {ŋ} would be cumbersome since the forms {g} and {k} could be spelled *g*, *k*, *q*, *x* or *c*. Rules for relating *c* to {k} and *x* to {ks} would have to be incorporated into this rule, along with the stress placement rules for *con-*, *in-*, and *syn-*.

(2) The first *p* in *sapphire* corresponds to {ø}.[15]
(3) *p* in all other cases corresponds to {p}.

c. *Alternations*

(1) Initial {p} in (*pn-*, *ps-*, *pt-*) corresponds to {ø}.
(2) In the medial combination *bilabial stop* + *bilabial stop*, the first stop is dropped.

ph

a. *Distribution*

ph is a relatively infrequent spelling in English although it occurs in initial, medial, and final position and in the clusters *phl-*, *phr-*, *sph-*, *phth-*, *-mph*, and *-lph*, as in *phlegm*, *phrase*, *sphere*, *phthisic*, *triumph*, and *sylph*.[16]

b. *Correspondences*

ph corresponds regularly to {f}.

c. *Alternations*

(1) {f} becomes {ø} in word initial position before {θ} (cf. *phthisic* and *diphthong*).
(2) {f} remains {f} in all other cases. (See also *Alternations* under *f*).

q

a. *Distribution*

q occurs only in initial and medial position, and in these positions

[15] The *pph* spelling in *sapphire* could be treated as a single compound consonant unit, akin to *tch* and *dg*. Since *sapphire* contains the only example of this cluster, however, the present treatment was adopted.
[16] *phl-* and *phth-* are rare clusters in English.

always before *u*. It also appears in the initial cluster *squ-*, e.g., *squirrel*, *squire*.

b. *Correspondences*

q corresponds regularly to {k}.

c. *Alternations*

None.

r

a. *Distribution*

r occurs in initial, medial, and final position and in a large number of clusters, the most common of which are shown below:

Initial *r* clusters

br-	brace	gr-	grade	spr-	spring
chr-	chrome	phr-	phrase	str-	strong
cr-	crash	pr-	prize	thr-	through
dr-	drive	scr-	screw	tr-	train
fr-	friend	shr-	shred	wr-	write

Final *r* clusters

-rb	herb	-rf	surf	-rn	urn
-rp	sharp	-rth	mirth	-rl	curl
-rd	bird	-rsh	marsh	-rpt	excerpt
-rt	smart	-rch	birch	-rst	first
-rg	berg	-rm	term	-rld	world

b. *Correspondences*

r in all cases corresponds to {r}. (On vowel + *r*, see Chapter VII).

c. *Alternations*

None.

rh

a. *Distribution*

The spelling *rh* is relatively rare, occurring in initial position before a vowel and medially and finally in the post vocalic cluster *rrh*, e.g., *rheostate*, *rhinoceros*, *cirrhosis*, *catarrh*.

b. *Correspondences*

*r*h corresponds regularly to {r}.

c. *Alternations*

None.

s

a. *Distribution*

s occurs in initial, medial and final position by itself, in a large number of initial consonant clusters, and in four monomorphemic final clusters. The initial and final clusters are shown below:

Initial Clusters

ps-	psychology	sl-	slow	squ-	squash
sc-	scare	sm-	small	st-	stand
sch-	school	sn-	snow	sth-	sthenic
schw-	schwa	sp-	special	str-	strong
scl-	sclerosis	sph-	sphere	sv-	svelte
scr-	scream	spl-	splash	sw-	swim
sk-	ski	spr-	spring		

Final Clusters

-sp	wasp	-sk	ask
-st	test	-rst	thirst

b. *Correspondences*

The correspondences for initial and final *s* are fairly regular; those for medial *s*, on the other hand, are highly irregular and cannot be predicted with any high degree of certainty. The rules which follow are not exhaustive and in some cases have as many exceptions as examples.

(1) *s* corresponds to {ø} in the following words:

aisle	apropos	chassis
corps	bourgeois	debris
demesne	challis	rendezvous
island	chamois	velours
isle		

(2) Final, inflectional *s* corresponds to {s}. The identity of inflectional *s*, however, must be retained on the morphophonemic level.
(3) Final *s* after a voiced consonant spelling and in *as*, *has*, *his*, *is*, *was* corresponds to {z}.
(4) Final *s* in all other cases corresponds to {s}.
(5) Initial *s* corresponds to {s}.
(6) Medial *s* before or after a voiceless consonant spelling and in the combinations *-ease-*, *-vowel* + *Cse* corresponds to {s} except in *cleanse* where it is {z}.
(7) *s* in all other cases corresponds to {z}.

c. *Alternations*

See also Chapter VI.

(1) Between an unstressed vowel and a stressed vowel, {s} corresponds to {z} (cf. *sign* : *design*, *solve* : *dissolve*, *sound* : *resound*).
(2) After {s, z, š, ž, č, ǰ} final morphemic {s} becomes {-ɪz}; after any other voiced morphophoneme it becomes {z}; otherwise, it remains as {s}.
(3) When the nouns *house* and *use*, and the adjective *close* are converted to verbs, {s} becomes {z}.

sh

a. *Distribution*

sh occurs alone in initial, medial, and final position, and in the monomorphemic clusters *shr-* and *-rsh* as in *shrimp* and *shroud*, *marsh* and *harsh.*

b. *Correspondences*

sh regularly corresponds to {š}.

c. *Alternations*

None.

t

a. *Distribution*

t occurs in initial, medial, and final position as a single consonant and in the following monomorphemic initial and final clusters.

Initial Clusters

pt-	ptomaine	tm-	tmesis
st-	storm	tr-	train
str-	strip	tw-	twenty

Final Clusters

-ct	pact	-mpt	attempt	-rst	first
-ft	left	-nct	distinct	-rt	smart
-ght	fought	-nt	rent	-st	must
-lct	mulct	-ntz	chintz	-tz	blitz
-lt	halt	-pt	apt	-xt	text
-ltz	waltz	-rpt	excerpt		

b. *Correspondences*

(1) *t* corresponds to {ø} in *depot*, *debut*, *hautboy*, *savant*, *mortgage*, and in words ending in *-et* with stress on the last syllable (e.g., *buffet*, *valet*).
(2) *t* in *equation* corresponds to {z}.
(3) In the combinations *t* + *vowel* + *vowel*, *t* corresponds to {s} when not preceded by *s* or *x* (cf. *nation* : *bastion*).
(4) *t* otherwise corresponds to {t}.

c. *Alternations*

(1) On the palatalization of {sj} to {š}, {zj} to {ž}, {tj} to {č}, and {dj} to {ǰ}, see Chapter VI.
(2) In the medial clusters {-Ct-} + $\left\{\begin{matrix}\text{-ən}\\ \text{-əl}\end{matrix}\right\}$, {t} corresponds to {ø}, e.g., *castle*, *often*.
(3) {t} otherwise corresponds to {t}.

th

a. *Distribution*

th occurs in initial, medial, and final position, and in the monomorphemic clusters *thr-* and *-rth*, as in *through*, *throw*, *birth*, and *north*. It also appears in the noun-clusters *sth-*:*sthenic*, *thw-*: *thwart*, and *-nth* : *labyrinth*.

b. *Correspondences*

(1) *th* in *thyme* corresponds to {t}.
(2) *th* in *isthmus* and *asthma* corresponds to {ø}.
(3) Initial *th* in functors corresponds to {ð}.[17]
(4) Medial *th* in the morpheme-final clusters, *-the* and *-ther* (except for *ether*) corresponds to {ð}.
(5) In *ether* and all other cases, *th* corresponds to {ð}.

[17] See Hocket, 1958, pp. 264-65, for a definition of functors.

c. *Alternations*

See also Chapter VI.
Non-productive alternations:[18]

{θ} — {ð}	north, northern
bath, baths	south, southern
breath, breathe	swath, swathe
cloth, clothe	teeth, teethe
mouth, mouths	worth, worthy

u

a. *Distribution*

u is a consonant spelling after *q*, (e.g., *quack*, *queen*, *acquire*), *g* (e.g., *guano*, *language*, *linguist*), and, exceptionally, after *s* as in *suave, persuade*. Except for *qu-* these spellings are rare in Modern English.

b. *Correspondences*

(1) Forms ending in *-que*, *-quet*, *-quette* and *quee* have *u* corresponding to {ø}.
(2) In *quay*, *queue*, *liquor*, *piquant*, *turquoise*, *u* corresponds to {ø}.
(3) In all other cases, consonantal *u* corresponds to {w}.

c. *Alternations*

None.

[18] There is also a tendency towards a {θ} — {ð} alternation in noun singular — noun plural, e.g., *bath*:*baths*, *moth*:*moths*. *path*:*paths*.

V

a. *Distributions*

Over 75 percent of all occurrences of *v* are found in medial positions in Modern English words; the remainder occur in initial positions. *v* rarely occurs in clusters with other consonants or in a geminate cluster (exceptions are *navvy*, *divvy*, and *flivver*).

b. *Correspondences*

v regularly corresponds to {v}.

c. *Alternations*

See also Chapter VI.
Non-productive alternations:

(a) {v} — {w}

vinter	wine

(b) Miscellaneous

deceive	deception
poverty	poor
receive	reception
revolve	revolution
solve	solution
weave	web

W

a. *Distribution*

w appears commonly in initial position before a vowel and in the clusters *wr-* as in *write* and *wrought*, *tw* as in *two* and *twine*, and *sw* as in *swan* and *sword.*

It occurs medially in *answer, award, aware, bewail, beware* and *reward, toward.*

b. *Correspondences*

(1) In *answer, sword, two,* and *toward, w* corresponds to {ø}.
(2) In all other cases *w* corresponds to {w}.

c. *Alternations*

For {v} — {w}, see non-productive alternations under *w*.

wh

a. *Distribution*

The spelling *wh-* occurs only in morpheme-initial position, as in *where, when, why.* It does not occur in clusters.

b. *Correspondences*

(1) *wh* in *who, whore* and *whole* corresponds to {h}.
(2) Elsewhere, *wh* corresponds to {hw-}.[19]

c. *Alternations*

None.

x

a. *Distribution*

x occurs chiefly in medial and final position, although it does appear initially in a number of scientific terms like *xenon, xenophobia,* and *xylem.* Consonant clusters with *x* do not occur in initial or final position, except for *lx*:*calx.*

[19] The dialectal variations of {hw}, {w} and {ʍ} are not treated here.

b. *Correspondences*

x corresponds regularly to {ks}.

c. *Alternations*

(1) Initially and between voiced morphophonemes, {ks} derived from *x* becomes {gz} if the preceding vowel is unstressed.[20]
(2) Initial {gz-} corresponds to {z}.

y

a. *Distribution*

As a consonant spelling *y* is relatively rare in Modern English, occurring in initial position in about one hundred words and in medial position in *beyond*, *canyon*, and in the suffix *-yer*, as in *lawyer* and *bowyer* (obsolete).

b. *Correspondences*

y corresponds regularly to {j}.

c. *Alternations*

None.

[20] Before this rule can be applied, the main word stress must be determined and {h} elision must take place. Otherwise, words like *exhaust* and *exhibit* would be handled incorrectly. Leveling of geminate consonant clusters, however, must not be done until after rule 1 is applied. That this rule does not apply to {ks} obtained from spellings other than *x* can be seen from the forms like *accept*, *accede*. On the palatalization of {sj} to {š} and {zj} to {ž} as in *luxury*:*luxurious*, see pp. 92ff. There are several exceptions to this rule, e.g., *doxology*, *luxation*, and *proximity*.

z

a. *Distribution*

z is the least frequently used letter in Modern English orthography, occurring in initial and medial position and less frequently in final position, as in *adz*, *chintz*, *quartz*, and *waltz*.[21] The only initial and final clusters it occurs in are *cz*:*czar*, *rtz*:*quartz*, *tz*:*blitz*, *ntz*:*chintz*, and *ltz*:*waltz*.

b. *Correspondences*

(1) *z* in final *tz* corresponds to {s}.
(2) Otherwise, *z* corresponds to {z}.

c. *Alternations*

See *Alternations*, under *s*.

tch, ck, dg

These three clusters share a number of features; each appears only after a checked vowel spelling, but in no monomorphemic final clusters, and each has a single morphophonemic correspondent. In addition, each was introduced in the early sixteenth century as a replacement for a geminate consonant cluster. *tch* replaced *cch*; *ck* replaced *cc* and *kk*; and *dg* replaced *gg* when it represented {ǰ}.

Correspondences[22]

tch corresponds to {č}, as in *kitchen, match.*
ck corresponds to {k}, as in *black, neck.*
dg corresponds to {ǰ}, as in *edge, midget.*

[21] Frequency counts for letters in English texts have appeared in Fletcher Pratt, *Secret and Urgent: the Story of Codes and Ciphers* (Indianapolis, 1939) and H. F. Gaines, *Cryptanalysis* (New York, 1939).

[22] From a theoretical standpoint, these three clusters do not have to be treated as separate units. Correspondences for *ck* can be handled by the correspondence rules given under *c* and *k*. For *tch* and *dg*, the rules for *t*, *d*, *ch*, and *g* can be applied, along with the rule for leveling geminate consonant clusters, given that {č} is represented as {tš} and {ǰ} as {dž}. Then *tch* and *dg* are mapped into {ttš} and {ddž} and these are later leveled to {tš} and {dž}.

Some forms like *exaggerate*, *account*, and *bacchanal* have retained Latin geminate clusters in spite of the general tendency in the sixteenth century to replace them with *tch*, *ck*, and *dg*.

gn, kh, sch

These three consonant units appear in a small number of borrowings; the words in which they occur and the correspondences for each are shown below:

gn

gn corresponds to {n} in *champagne*
gn corresponds to {nj} in *lorgnette*, *mignon*, *mignonette*, *poignant* and *vignette*

kh

kh corresponds to {k} in *khan* and *khaki*

sch

sch corresponds to {s} in *schism*
sch corresponds to {š} in *schist* and *schwa.*

VI

FRICATIVE ALTERNATIONS

1. PALATALIZATION

a. *Phonetic Process*

The process of palatalization (often called assibilation) accounts for many so-called irregular spelling-to-sound correspondences which involve the spellings *d*, *s*, *t*, *x*, *z* and the vowels which follow them in certain environments.

> Under this name (assibilation) it is convenient here to comprise two changes, /sj/ and /zj/ < (š, ž), and /tj/ and /dj/ < (tš, dž). In the first we have a sort of complete assimilation of the two sounds. In the second change, the off-glide from the more or less palatalized stop /t, d/ had developed into the sibilant, which has in most cases absorbed the following /j/.[1]

Kenyon (1943, p. 135), in what is probably the best summary to be found of the phonetics of this process, describes two phonetic tendencies which lead to palatalization. The first is the shift of unaccented /ɪ/ before another vowel to /j/, so that the number of syllables in the word is reduced by one. Then, through assimilation, the changes /sj, zj, tj, dj/ — /š, ž, č, ǰ/ occur. In the model used in this paper, palatalization is described as a morphophonemic process. Thus, {sj, zj, tj, dj} become {š, ž, č, ǰ} in certain environments.

The palatalizing {j} is derived from several independent sources. In *creature*, for example, *u* is mapped directly into {ju};

[1] Jespersen, 1909, I, 341.

in *cordial*, however, *i* is mapped first into {ɪ}, and then unstressed {ɪ} + vowel becomes {j} + vowel (with some exceptions). Palatalization generally takes place before an unstressed vowel; compare, for example, the stress on *u* in the following lists:

Palatalized	*Unpalatalized*
credulous	credulity
cynosure	pursuit
capitulate	presume
schedule	importune
assiduous	assiduity
treasure	institute

b. *Morphophonemic rules for palatalization*

(1) {sj} + (unstressed vowel) → {š} + (vowel)
(2) {zj} + (unstressed vowel) → {ž} + (vowel)
(3) {tj} + (unstressed vowel) → {č} + (vowel)
(4) {dj} + (unstressed vowel) → {ǰ} + (vowel)

Examples:

luxury → {luksjurɪ} → {lə́kšurɪ}
azure → {æzjur} → {ǽzjər} → {ǽžər}
creature → {kritjur} → {krítjər} → {kríčər}
cordial → {kordɪal} → {kórdjəl} → {kórǰəl}

Exceptions:

sure, *sugar*, *mature*, *produce*(ⁿ).

2. VOICED-VOICELESS ALTERNATIONS

The morphophonemic alternations {s-z}, {f-v}, {θ-ð}, {š-ž} reveal a number of problems in the construction of a model for spelling-to-sound correspondences. These problems, though encountered here in traversing from the orthography toward sound, also occur in the construction of other models for English morphophonemics, so that the considerations presented below have a much wider significance than in spelling-to-sound studies alone. In the discussion which follows it is assumed that spellings have been mapped onto an initial morphophonemic level and the next objective is to describe alternations in terms of regular and irregular rules. For this section, an alternation that is both productive and frequent is labeled REGULAR. All others are IRREGULAR. The specific problems which are discussed in relation to the voiceless-voiced alternations are:

(1) generalizations which can be made about these alternations.
(2) relevant differences which exist among the non-productive (irregular) patterns.

Whether or not an alternation is marked in the orthography is relevant for both reading and spelling. This fact will be mentioned for each pattern, but not discussed thoroughly.

Summary of the Alternations

(I) Noun plural {s-z(ɪz)} *cats* : *dogs*(*horses*) (unmarked)
(II) Noun-adjective
  (a) {š–ž} *luxury* : *luxurious* (unmarked)
  (b) {s–z} *louse* : *lousy* (unmarked)
  (c) {θ–ð} *north* : *northern* (unmarked)
(III) Verb-verb
  {s–z} *sound* : *resound* (unmarked)
(IV) Noun-verb (infinitive)
  (a) {f–v} *belief* : *believe* (marked)
  (b) {θ–ð} *breath* : *breathe* (marked)
  (c) {s–z}
    (1) *house* (n.) : *house* (v.) (unmarked)
    (2) *glass* : *glaze* (marked)
(V) Noun singular-noun plural
  (a) {f–v} *wife* : *wives* (marked)
  (b) {θ–ð} *bath* : *baths* (unmarked)
  (c) {s–z} *house* : *houses* (unmarked)
(VI) Verb (past)-verb (present)
  {f–v} *left* : *leave* (marked)

(VII) Noun-noun
{θ–ð} *smith* : *smithy* (dialectal) (unmarked)
(VIII) Ordinal-cardinal
{f–v} *fifth* : *five* (marked)

Of these alternations, only a few are invariant. The noun plural (I) certainly is. It is a phonetically conditioned alternation which is describable by a single rule. It is generally not marked in the spelling, as shown by the following plurals, all of which add only *s* to the singular:

houses {hauzɪz}
boys {bɔɪz}
cats {kæts}

(Where *-es* is added for the plural, the alternate {ɪz} is marked).

Class VIII, the ordinal-cardinal alternations, is also invariant since the only two members which end in voiced {v} in the cardinal have unvoiced {f} in the ordinal, viz., *five* : *fifth*, *twelve* : *twelfth*. One rule for generation of the ordinal forms from the cardinal forms, therefore, can be stated as:

final, cardinal {v} → ordinal {f}.

It is also possible to state this rule as follows:

final voiced fricative (cardinal) → unvoiced fricative (ordinal)

because no other cardinals end in a voiced fricative. Such a generalization, however, is probably not acceptable unless there are other major patterns in the orthography which show a voiced-voiceless alternation for fricatives. The existence of such patterns beyond the noun plural are explored in the remainder of this section.

Class IV b, the {θ-ð} alternation in noun-verb, is nearly invariant, but since it has so few examples, there is a temptation to base its classification upon those of the other class IV alternations. The nouns which end in {θ} and which can also be used as verbs are the following:

{θ-ð}		{θ-θ}	
n.	v.	n.	v.
breath	breathe	froth	froth
cloth	clothe	earth	(un)earth
mouth	mouth		
swath	swathe		
teeth	teethe		

The {f-v} alternations for noun-verb are not nearly so regularas, the following lists demonstrate.

{f-v}		{f-f}	
n.	v.	n.	v.
belief	believe	brief	brief
grief	grieve	dwarf	dwarf
half	halve	leaf	leaf
life	live	sniff	sniff
proof	prove	spoof	spoof
relief	relieve	stuff	stuff
shelf	shelve	whiff	whiff
thief	thieve		

It would be stretching a point considerably to state that in general nouns ending in {f} change {f} to {v} in forming the corresponding infinitive. At best, it can be said that there is a class of nouns (which must be enumerated in the lexicon attached to the model) in which the voiceless-voiced alternation occurs for this production.

The case for an {s-z} alternation in this class is even more tenuous. *Abuse*, *grease* (dialectically), *house*, and *use* have this alternation, as do, in an extended sense, *brass* (*braze*), *glass* (*glaze*), and *grass* (*graze*). But there is an even longer list of forms like *class*, *curse*, *dress*, *eclipse*, *glimpse*, *mass*, *nurse*, *pass*, *press*, *stress*, and *witness* in which no such alternation occurs. In general, nouns ending in {s} do not change {s} to {z} in forming the corresponding infinitive.

On the basis of this evidence there is no justification for establishing a regular voiceless-voiced alternation for this class. This indicates, furthermore, that no special status should be assigned to the {θ-ð} alternation, even though it occurs in five of the seven possible cases. The only conclusion that can be drawn is that nouns ending in voiceless fricatives generally retain the voiceless quality in forming the infinitive. There is, however, a productive subpattern in which the voiceless fricative becomes voiced.

Class II a, which has only one example in the corpus used for this study, and probably not very many more in all of the English language, might also be classed as regular. But this depends upon whether the alternation {ks} → {gz} is classed as regular or not. If spelling is used as the starting point, then this is possible, but not necessarily desirable. Intervocalic *x* could be mapped into $\{k_x s_x\}$ and then a stress rule applied to convert $\{k_x s_x\}$ to {gz}: $\{k_x s_x\}$ → {gz} when the primary stress is not on the preceding vowel, cf. *execute*:*exist*. {ks} derived from *x*, here labeled $\{k_x s_x\}$, must be distinguished from {ks}, derived from *cc*, since {ks} derived from *cc* does not become {gz} under any circumstances (cf. *access* : *accessible*, *accept* : *acceptable*). Under the classifications of *x*-derived {ks} and *cc*-derived {ks}, the {š-ž} alternation in *luxury* : *luxurious* is regular; the actual alternation, however, is not {š-ž}, but {s-z}. {š} and {ž} result from the palatalizations {sj} → {š} and {zj} → {ž}. This means first that the alternation {š-ž} is, from the standpoint of a generative model, actually the alternation {s-z} and second, that it is regular only if the identity of *x*- derived {ks} is maintained until after stress is applied. If this identity is not maintained, then there is no reason to call {ks} → {gz} regular. In lieu of the lack of other criteria to apply, frequency favors the invariantly voiceless cluster: *accent* : *accentuate*, *accept* : *acceptable*, *access* : *accessible*, *accident* : *accidental*. Therefore, the alternation in *luxury* : *luxurious* is not classed as regular here.

Class III could, and probably should, be designated as regular. The members of this class are:

sign, design (resign, etc.)
solve, dissolve (absolve, resolve, etc.)
sound, resound.

The rule is that initial {s} becomes {z} when a prefix ending in an unstressed vowel is added.

Class V is the largest of the remaining classes, containing the following pairs:

{s-z}	{f-v}	{θ-ð}
house, houses	calf, calves	bath, baths
	elf, elves	cloth, cloths
	half, halves	lath, laths
	knife, knives	moth, moths
	leaf, leaves	mouth, mouths
	life, lives	path, paths
	loaf, loaves	wreath, wreaths
	self, selves	(Most of the plurals
	sheaf, sheaves	above vary between
	shelf, shelves	{θ} and {ð}. The
	staff, staves	dialect distribution
	thief, thieves	for this alternation
	wife, wives	has not been fully
	wolf, wolves	determined).

The lack of a {š-ž} alternation and the rarity of the {s-z} alternation eliminate the possibilty of a general voicing rule for final fricatives in forming the noun plural. This leaves the possibility of labeling the {f-v} and {θ-ð} alternations as regular. But the regular label implies either that there is a phonetic or grammatical factor that will allow the prediction of the alternation, or that this alternation occurs with a high frequency. That the {f-v} or {θ-ð} alternations are not phonetically or grammatically predictable can be seen from the following items:

gulf	gulfs	breath	breaths	month	months
reef	reefs	width	widths	earth	earths

The frequency question also is answered in the negative, although the {f-v} alternation does occur in almost one-third of the nouns which end in final {f}. The remainder retain {f} in forming the plural. This would imply that the *leaf*: *leaves* alternation should be classed as irregular, just as is the petrified alternation represented by *smith* : *smithy*. Our native speaker's intuition, however, is uncomfortable with this solution.

The *smith* : *smithy* alternation is not only uncommon, but also would be rarely invoked as a model for forming new English words. *Leaf* : *leaves* on the other hand, appears more productive. We know, for example, that voiced fricative plurals of such words as *dwarf* and *roof* occur in American speech. Furthermore, the formation of the noun plural from the noun singular is one of the most common forms of word formation in English. Formation of one noun from another by the addition of *y* is much less productive.

The issue here is that a model that concerns itself strictly with regular and irregular categories fails to account for some features of the language. While much work remains to be done, the tentative decision is to subdivide the irregular class into *productive* and *petrified* subclasses. At best, alternations like *leaf* : *leaves* fit into the *productive-irregular* class while those like *smith*:*smithy* fit into the *petrified-irregular* group.

Finally, it should be noted that all {f-v} alternations are marked in the orthography by change in the functional unit, while in the {s-z} alternations only the petrified alternation represented by *glass* : *glaze* is marked (also by a change of functional unit), and in the {θ-ð} alternations, only the noun-verb one is marked, and this by addition of the final *e* marker which is the only possible device for marking the voiced pronunciation of *th*.

A reclassification of these alternations, based upon the newly adopted classes, is shown below:

REGULAR

(1)	noun plural	{s-z (-Iz)}	*cats* : *dogs*
(2)	verb-verb	{s-z}	*sound* : *resound*
(3)	ordinal-cardinal	{f-v}	*fifth* : *five*

IRREGULAR

Productive

(1)	noun-adjective	{θ-ð}	*north* : *northern*
(2)	noun-verb	{θ-ð}	*breath* : *breathe*

	{f-v}	*belief* : *believe*
	{s-z}	*house* (n.) : *house* (v.)
(3) noun singular-noun plural	{f-v}	*wife* : *wives*
	{θ-ð}	*bath* : *baths*
	{s-z}	*house* : *houses*
Petrified		
(1) noun-adjective	{s-z}	*louse* : *lousy*
		luxury : *luxurious*
(2) noun-verb	{s-z}	*glass* : *glaze*
(3) verb (past)-verb (present)	{f-v}	*left* : *leave*
(4) noun-noun	{θ-ð}	*smith* : *smithy*
		thief : *thieve* (but *theft*)

VII

VOWEL DISTRIBUTIONS, CORRESPONDENCES, AND ALTERNATIONS

1. PRIMARY VOWEL PATTERNS

a. *Introduction*

The vowel spellings *a*, *e*, *i*/*y*, *o*, *u*, called primary vowel spellings in this paper, carry the major burden of vowel representation in the current orthography.[1] They occur in all positions and have a vast complexity of morphophonemic correspondences and alternations which reflect an even more complex history. When viewed from the direct spelling-to-sound standpoint, the patterns for these units reveal no regularity. *o* corresponds to seventeen different sounds, *a* to ten, *e* to nine, and the combined group to forty-eight. When the morphemic structure and consonant environments of the words in which these units appear are analyzed, however, a single major pattern emerges, from which regular sub-patterns can be derived. Exceptions still remain, large numbers of them in some cases, but the underlying pattern is so dominating that the exceptions, which were once the rule, become mere oddities, begging for historical justification. In the discussion which follows the major pattern for the stressed vowels is introduced in a general form and then refined through the introduction of its regular sub-patterns, alternations and exceptions.[2]

[1] Henceforth *i* will stand for both *i* and *y*.

[2] Word stress patterns play a significant role in the relationship of spelling to sound, especially in the correspondences of the primary vowel spellings. With a few exceptions, only stressed vowels are treated in this paper. Three levels of stress, all introduced on the morphophonemic level, are assumed:

b. *Major Patterns*

Each of the primary vowel units corresponds regularly to two different morphophonemes, a checked one and a free one, according to the morphemic structure of the word in which it occurs and the consonant and vowel units which follow it. These correspondences are shown in Table 1.[3]

TABLE 1

Major Pattern for Primary Vowels

Spelling	Free Alternate	Checked Alternate
a	{e}	{æ}
	s*a*ne	s*a*nity
	m*a*te	m*a*t
	r*a*tion	r*a*ttle
e	{i}	{ɛ}
	athl*e*te	athl*e*tic
	m*e*te	m*e*t
	p*e*nal	p*e*nnant
i	{ai}	{ɪ}
	r*i*se	r*i*sen
	mal*i*gn	mal*i*gnant
	s*i*te	s*i*t
o	{o}	{a}
	c*o*ne	c*o*nic
	r*o*be	r*o*b
	p*o*sy	p*o*ssible
u	{ju}[4]	{ə}
	ind*u*ce	ind*u*ction
	r*u*de	r*u*dder
	l*u*cre	l*u*xury

primary, secondary, and tertiary (unstressed). While some forms of English word stress are "predictable", no extensive analysis of this topic has ever been published. Two recent publications, however, indicate that work is being done in this area. See George S. Waldo, "The Significant of Accentuation in English Words", *Proceedings of the Ninth International Congress of Linguists* (The Hague, 1964), pp. 204-10, and Roger Kingdon, *The Groundwork of English Stress* (London, 1958).

[3] For exceptions to this pattern, stated as direct spelling-to-sound correspondences, see Wijk, pp. 26-41.

[4] The retention or elision of {j} before {u} is handled as a morphophonemic process.

In monomorphemic words a primary spelling unit corresponds to its free alternate when it is followed by (1) a functionally simple consonant unit which in turn is followed by another vowel unit (including final *e*) or (2) a functionally simple consonant unit, followed by *l* or *r*, and then another vowel unit (including final *e*).[5] It corresponds to its checked alternate in the remaining cases, i.e., when followed by (1) a functionally compound consonant unit, e.g., *x*, *dg*, (2) a cluster of consonant units, e.g., *-nn*, *lth* or, (3) a word-final consonant unit or units. Examples of these correspondences are shown in Table 2. The column numbers correspond to the numbered qualifications in the sentences above.

TABLE 2

Examples of Primary Vowel Correspondences for Selected Environments

Spelling	Free Alternate		Checked Alternate		
	1	2	1	2	3
a	c*a*nine	l*a*dle	b*a*dge	s*a*ddle	s*a*t
e	m*e*dian	z*e*bra	*e*xit	ant*e*nna	*e*bb
i	p*i*lot	m*i*crobe	ch*i*cken	ep*i*stle	h*i*tch
o	v*o*gue	n*o*ble	p*o*cket	c*o*gnate	s*o*d
u	d*u*bious	l*u*cre	l*u*xury	s*u*pper	r*u*g

A simple vowel spelling, followed by a simple consonant spelling and then *le*, corresponds to its free alternate, e.g., *table*. But a geminate consonant cluster before the *le* marks the checked alternate, e.g., *apple*.

[5] The difference between monomorphemic and polymorphemic words, a difference unfortunately neglected in the teaching of reading, is too complex to be discussed adequately here. For the prediction of sound from spelling in a large number of words, however, the distinction is crucial. What are involved, primarily, are the morphophonemic alternations which occur with suffixation, as in /ə́rben/ : /ərbǽnɪtɪ/, /kon/ : /kánɪk/. On this topic, see Stanley S. Newman, "English Suffixation: A Descriptive Approach", *Word* 4 (1948), 24-36. For a pedagogical approach to suffixation, see Edward L. Thorndike, *The Teaching of English Suffixes* (New York, 1941).

TABLE 3

The le Pattern

a	ladle	addle
e	——	pebble
i	rifle	riffle
o	noble	cobble
u	ruble	rubble

This pattern has a limited distribution. Only *b, p, t, f, g,* and *ng* occur more than once before final *le,* and of these, only *b, p, d, t,* and *f* double in this position, (*s* and *x* occur before *le* in *measles* and *axle, ss* occurs in *tussle*). *Treble,* an exception for the pronunciation of *e,* is the only example in Modern English of the spelling *e* + C + *le* (final).

The correspondences for these vowel spellings in polymorphemic words depends not only upon the graphemic environment, but also in many cases upon the morphemic structure of the word.

c. *Sub-Patterns*

The two most important sub-patterns which can be derived from the major pattern are the final *e* pattern and the geminate consonant pattern. Examples of these are shown in Table 4. Complete analyses are given in the two following sections.

TABLE 4

Examples of Final e *and Geminate Consonant Patterns*

Spelling	Final *e* Pattern	Geminate Consonant Pattern
a	r*a*te — r*a*t	*a*nal — *a*nnals
e	m*e*te — m*e*t	P*e*ter — p*e*tter
i	s*i*te — s*i*t	d*i*ner — d*i*nner
o	p*o*pe — p*o*p	c*o*ma — c*o*mma
u	c*u*te — c*u*t	s*u*per — s*u*pper

d. *Final* e *Pattern*

While the final *e* pattern applies primarily to monosyllabic words, it also holds for many polysyllabic words, even when the vowel before the final *e* is unstressed, as in *microbe, decade, schedule, volume, placate.* Besides the patterns mentioned above (*vowel + consonant + e, vowel + consonant + le, vowel + consonant + re*), the environment *vowel + ste* is also part of the final *e* pattern, as in *baste, chaste* and *haste.* Examples of regular correspondences are shown below, followed by an exhaustive list of exceptions for stressed vowels.

TABLE 5

Examples of the Final e *Pattern*

a → {e}	*i* → {ai}	*u* → {ju}	*e* → {i}	*o* → {o}
b*a*ke	c*y*cle	c*u*be	acc*e*de	c*o*ve
dec*a*de	domic*i*le	d*u*ke	imp*e*de	er*o*de
f*a*ble	f*i*ve	m*u*le	obsol*e*te	gl*o*be
g*a*ge	pr*i*ze	prod*u*ce	sch*e*me	j*o*ke
h*a*ste	prof*i*le	res*u*me	ser*e*ne	medi*o*cre
sh*a*ke	subl*i*me	sec*u*re	th*e*me	sm*o*ke

e. *Irregular Correspondences for the Final* e *Pattern*

(1) *a* corresponds to {æ} in *bade, forbade, have, morale. a* corresponds to {a} in *are, barrage, camouflage, corsage, facade, garage, massage, mirage, sabotage.* NOTE: *a* in the ending *-ate* corresponds to {e} in verbs, but alternates to {ɪ} in nouns and adjectives. Cf. *duplicate* (vb.) : *duplicate* (adj., noun). (The stress patterns are also different in these forms).

(2) *e* corresponds to {ɛ} in *allege, clientele, ere, there, treble, where.*[6]
e corresponds to {ɪ} in *renege.*
e corresponds to {ə} in *were.*
e corresponds to {i} in *fete.*

(3) *i* corresponds to {i} in the following words:

bast*i*le[7] mach*i*ne rav*i*ne val*i*se

[6] In the following words final *e* is not a marker, but a relational unit, (1) corresponding to {ɪ}: *adobe, coyote, epitome, extempore, facsimile, finale, hyperbole, nike, recipe, sesame, simile, ukulele,* (2) corresponding to {e}: *cafe, protege.*

[7] *Bastile* is an alternate spelling of *bastille.*

capr*i*ce	mar*i*ne	reg*i*me
el*i*te	pol*i*ce	rout*i*ne
	prest*i*ge	sard*i*ne
		tanger*i*ne

i corresponds to {ɪ} in *give* and *live*. NOTE: The spelling *i* is highly irregular in the ending *-ine* when it does not receive the primary word stress. Cf. *canine*, *asinine* : *examine*, *famine*.

(4) *o* corresponds to {ə} in *above*, *come*, *done*, *dove*, *glove*, *love*, *none*, *shove*, *some*.
o corresponds to {u} in *lose*, *move*, *prove*, *whose*.
o corresponds to {ɔ} in *gone*.

f. *Vowel Spellings before Geminate Consonants*

The primary spellings *a*, *e*, *i*, *o*, *u* occur frequently before geminate consonants, the digraph (secondary) spellings, rarely.[8] (The French

[8] Except for the Spanish borrowing *llama*, geminate consonants occur only in medial and final position in English spelling. The most common final clusters are *ff*, *ll*, and *ss* as in *fluff*, *mill* and *toss*. Rare final clusters are *bb*, *dd*, *gg*, *nn*, *rr*, *tt*, and *zz*, which occur only in the words, *ebb*, *add*, *odd*, *egg*, *inn*, *err*, *burr*, *purr*, *whirr*, *boycott*, *butt*, *putt*, *watt*, *buzz*, *fizz*, *fuzz*, *jazz*, *razz*. In medial position the following are common:

bb	cabbage, lobby	*mm*	comment, summit
cc	broccoli, occupy	*nn*	annals, dinner
dd	addict, eddy	*pp*	copper, happy
ff	coffee, giraffe	*rr*	error, surrey
gg	luggage, nugget	*ss*	blossom, gossip
ll	fillet, pillow	*tt*	button, clutter

vv and *zz* also occur medially, but only in *divvy*, *flivver*, *navvy*, *blizzard*, *dizzy*. No other geminate clusters occur, although *dg*, *ck*, and *tch* can be considered as geminate substitutes.

Consonant gemination also occurs when certain suffixes are added to words ending in a single consonant. For example, *run*: *running*, *forbid:forbidding*, *abet:abetted*. The orthographic rule is usually stated as follows:

> Monosyllables and words accented on the last syllable, when ending in a single consonant, *b*, *d*, *f*, *g*, *k*, *l*, *m*, *n*, *p*, *r*, *s*, *t*, *v* preceded by a single vowel, double the consonant before adding a termination beginning with a vowel or the suffix *-y*. *Webster's*, 1856, p. 1145.

Exceptions to this rule are plentiful and usage is still unsettled on whether or not to double final *l*. For a colorful survey of eighteenth and nineteenth century grammatical literature on this topic, see Goold Brown's, *Grammar of English Grammars* (4th ed. New York, 1859), pp. 198-200.

The non-gemination of *v* and *th* has led to a large number of exceptions to the major pattern for the correspondences of the primary vowel spellings. *Cover*, borrowings, *braille*, *chauffeur*, and *trousseau* are the only examples from the corpus used for this study). Before geminate consonant clusters, primary vowel spellings correspond to their checked alternates, with the following exceptions:

(1) *a* in *mamma* corresponds to {a} and *a* in *marshmallow* corresponds to {ɛ}.

(2) *o* in *across*, *albatross*, and *boss* and before *ff* corresponds to {ɔ}.

(3) *o* in *gross*, and before final *ll* (except for *doll*), corresponds to {o}.

(4) *u* in *butte* corresponds to {ju} and *u* in *pudding* and *pussy* corresponds to {ʊ}.

TABLE 6

Examples of Regular Correspondences Before Geminate Consonants

a → {æ}	e → {ɛ}	i → {ɪ}	o → {a}	u → {ə}
*a*bbess	app*e*llate	art*i*llery	acc*o*mmodate	b*u*tton
*a*ccent	b*e*ggar	bac*i*llus	c*o*llar	f*u*nnel
*a*pple	b*e*llow	bl*i*zzard	c*o*llege	f*u*nny
b*a*bbittry	c*e*llar	cr*i*bbage	c*o*mma	h*u*llabaloo
c*a*bbage	ch*e*ddar	*i*ssue	c*o*mmerce	h*u*mmock
c*a*llow	dil*e*mma	m*i*llion	d*o*llar	m*u*mmy
f*a*llacy	*e*bb	shr*i*ll	h*o*bby	p*u*ddle
fl*a*bby	f*e*llow	s*y*mmetry	h*o*llow	p*u*mmel
gr*a*mmar	k*e*nnel	van*i*lla	l*o*bby	r*u*bber
h*a*ppen	l*e*sson	v*i*llage	s*o*nnet	sh*u*tter
m*a*mmal	m*e*ssage	w*i*llow	tob*o*ggan	s*u*pper
r*a*ttle	t*e*nnis	wr*i*ggle	t*o*ggle	t*u*nnel

bevel, *level*, *river*, *brother*, *mother*, *other*, for example, have vowel spellings corresponding to checked alternates in environments which indicate free alternates. To indicate the checked alternate, *v* and *th* would have to be geminated, but the graphotactical patterns of English exclude the doubling of these units. In *prison*, a slightly different problem exists. While *ss*, which is needed to make the correspondence *i* — {ɪ}, is allowed, it generally corresponds to {s} in medial position, as in *blossom*, *gossip*, and *lasso*, so it could not be employed where *s* corresponds to {z}. The present use of *ss* is derived from old French orthography where "intervocalic *ss* served to distinguish voiceless *s* from voiced *s* (= z)." Alfred Ewert, *The French Language* (London, 1933), p. 113.

2. ALTERNATIONS BASED UPON PRIMARY VOWEL SPELLINGS

The major pattern for the primary vowel spellings in stressed positions depends upon two basic features: environment, which was discussed in the previous sections, and morphemic structure, which is discussed briefly in this and the following sections. Morphemic structure forms the basis for describing the morphophonemic alternations based upon the primary vowel spellings. For example, the word *sanity*, if considered solely on the basis of the rules given in the preceding section, would be an exception to the major pattern since *a* before a simple consonant unit followed by a vowel corresponds to its checked rather than to its free alternate. If viewed, however, in relation to the sequences, *sane* : *sanity*, *humane* : *humanity*, and *urbane* : *urbanity*, another regular feature can be seen. By starting with the forms *sane*, *humane*, and *urbane*, regular rules can be written for changing the free alternate {e} to the checked alternate {æ} when the suffix *-ity*: {-ɪtɪ} is added.

This rule also holds for the spellings *e*, *i* and *o*, as can be seen from the following examples:

e	extr*e*me	extr*e*mity
	obsc*e*ne	obsc*e*nity
	ser*e*ne	ser*e*nity
i	asin*i*ne	asin*i*nity
	div*i*ne	div*i*nity
	mal*i*gn	mal*i*gnity
	sen*i*le	sen*i*lity
o	friv*o*lous	friv*o*lity
	medi*o*cre	medi*o*crity
	prec*o*cious	prec*o*city
	verb*o*se	verb*o*sity

(Morphophonemic alternations based upon stressed *u* are rare in Modern English, the most common being those which occur in *assume* : *assumption*, *conduce* : *conduction*, *presume* : *presumption*, *reduce* : *reduction*. Even with loss of stress *u*: {ju} tends not to change to {ə}. Thus, *compute* : *computation*, *execute* : *execution*, *usurer* : *usurious*, *utilize* : *utility*).

While a complete survey of vowel morphophonemics is beyond the scope of this paper, some of the more common alternations are presented below:

(1) *-ic*:		*free — checked*	
	a	*a*ngel	*a*ngelic
		st*a*te	st*a*tic
	e	athl*e*te	athl*e*tic
		hygi*e*ne	hygi*e*nic
		m*e*ter	m*e*tric
	i	c*y*cle	c*y*clic
		m*i*me	m*i*mic
		paral*y*ze	paral*y*tic
	o	c*o*ne	c*o*nic
		neur*o*sis	neur*o*tic
		ph*o*ne	ph*o*nic
(2) *-ion*		*free — checked*	
	e	conc*e*de	conc*e*ssion
		conv*e*ne	conv*e*ntion
	i	coll*i*de	coll*i*sion
		dec*i*de	dec*i*sion
		prov*i*de	prov*i*sion

3. CONSONANT INFLUENCES

r

a. *Introduction*

Post-vocalic /r/ is the source of not only a wide variation of vowel pronunciations across dialects, but also a complex and in some places, irregular development of spelling-to-sound correspondences. The selection of transcriptions of post-vocalic /r/ words is, in some cases, arbitrary. One speaker may alternate freely between such forms as /ziro/ and /zɪro/, /mɛri/ and /meri/ and /born/ and /bɔrn/. Some speakers contrast *horse* : *hoarse*, *for* : *four*, *marry* : *merry* : *Mary*, and some do not.[9] In the transcriptions

[9] See Kenyon, 1958, pp. 110-12.

used for this paper, /e/ and /i/ have coalesced with tautosyllabic /ɛ/ and /ɪ/. Intra-dialectal variation between /a/ and /o/ and between /ɔ/ and /o/ is indicated by a/o and ɔ/o (either morphophonemic or phonemic), as in *orange*, *origin*, *forest*, *glory*, *moron*, *orient*, and the syllabic peak in words like *bird*, *word*, and *urge* is symbolized phonemically (and morphophonemically) as /-ər/; e.g., *bird* /bərd/, *word* /wərd/, *urge* /ərǰ/.[10]

b. *Correspondences*

The correspondences of a primary vowel spelling before tautosyllabic *r* depends upon the environment following *r*. Three cases must be considered:

(1) *r* followed by a vowel unit, which in turn is followed by a vowel unit or juncture.
(2) *r* followed by a vowel unit, which in turn is followed by a consonant, or *r* followed by *r*.
(3) *r* followed by a consonant or juncture.

The morphophonemic correspondences for the primary vowel spellings are shown below. Environments 1, 2 and 3 refer to the descriptions just given. The *r* columns contain the correspondences for the vowels before *r*; the *normal* column contains the correspondences normally anticipated for that environment.

TABLE 7

Vowel Correspondences Before r

Spelling	Environment 1		Environment 2		Environment 3	
	r	normal	*r*	normal	*r*	normal
a	ɛ	e	æ	æ	a	æ
e	ɪ	i	ɛ	ɛ	ə	ɛ
i	aɪ	aɪ	ɪ	ɪ	ə	ɪ
o	ɔ/o	o	a/o	a	o/ɔ	a
u	ju	ju	ə	ə	ə	ə

[10] See Ilse Lehiste, *Acoustical Characteristics of Selected English Consonants* (= *IJAL* Publication No. 34) (Bloomington, Indiana, 1964), pp. 51-115.

EXAMPLES

Environment 1

a beware, malaria, nefarious, secretary
e adhere, cereal, exterior, sphere
i dire, enquiry, hire, wire
o adore, glory, more, shore
u bureau, cure, mature, spurious

Environment 2

a arid, arrogate, marriage, tariff
e austerity, errand, peril, terrace
i empiric, irrigate, miracle, mirror
o borrow, foreign, horrid, orange
u burr, current, furrier, hurry

Environment 3

a alarm, carve, gargle, star
e erb, erst, her, infer
i bird, girl, virtue, whirl
o adorn, formula, or, storm
u cur, spur, urge, urn

EXCEPTIONS

Environment 1

a are, aria, safari
e very
i delirium
u bury

Environment 2

a alarum, catarrh, harem
e err
i iris, irony, siren, spiral, squirrel, stirrup, tirade, virus
o borough, thorough, worry
u mural, urine

Environment 3

a scarce
e concerto, sergeant
o attorney

l

Correspondences

Before final *-ll* and medial or final *-l* plus another consonant, *a* corresponds not to {æ}, but to {ɔ} as in *almanac*, *alternation*, *call*, *chalk*, *mall*, *psalm*, and *walk*.[11] This shift does not occur before medial *ll*, however. Compare, for example, the following: *call*: *calliper*; *fall*: *fallacy*; *gall*: *gallow*; *hall*: *hallow*; *mall*: *mallard*; *tall*: *tallow*. In addition, *o* before final *-ll* or medial *l* plus consonant corresponds to {o} rather than to {a}.[12] Thus,

bold	polka	boll : bollard
folk	scold	poll : pollen
jolt	told	roll : rollick
molt	yolk	troll : trolley

That no other consonants are influenced by *-ll* can be seen from the following examples:

bell : bellow	fill : filly
fell : fellow	bull : bullet
bill : billion	gull : gullet

4. *W* INFLUENCE

With the exception of the *a* + *l* patterns discussed above, *a* preceded by initial *w* in a checked environment corresponds to {æ} before spelling for velars ({k, g, ŋ}) and to {a} otherwise. Compare, for example, *wad*, *waffle*, *wander*, *wasp*: *wax*, *wag*, *waggle*,

[11] Some exceptions are *alkali*, *altitude*, *contralto* and *palmetto*.
[12] Exceptions are *dolphin*, *olfactory*, *revolve*, *solve* and *volcano*.

wangle. With many of the *w* + *a* words there is considerable dialectal variation (e.g., *want*, *wash*, *water*).

o + *r* preceded by *w* corresponds to {ər}, except for *worn* which has o → {o}.

5. MISCELLANEOUS CONSONANT INFLUENCES

i before final *nd*, *ld*, and *gn*/*gm* corresponds to its free alternate {aɪ} rather than its checked alternate {ɪ}.

-nd	behind	grind	remind
	bind	hind	rind
	blind	kind	wind (v.)
	find	mind	
-ld	child, mild, wild (but gild)		
-gn	align	design	
	assign	malign	
	benign	resign	
	consign	sign	
-gm	paradigm		

o before final *ld* corresponds to its free alternate {o} rather than its checked alternate {a}.

bold	old
fold	scold
hold	sold
mold	

gh

Of the simple vowel spellings, only *i* occurs before *gh*, and in this environment *i* corresponds invariably to {aɪ} and *gh* to {ø}.

Examples

blight	light	thigh
fight	right	tight
flight	sigh	
high	slight	

Of the compound vowel spellings, *ai*, *au*, *ei*, and *ou* occur before *gh*, but the correspondences for these vowels or for *gh* in these environments are not entirely predictable. Shown below are the correspondences for each compound vowel, along with exhaustive word listings from the research corpus for each correspondence.

ai	→	{e}	straight		
au	→	{æ}	draught, laugh		
au	→	{ɔ}	caught	naughty	taught
			daughter	naught	
			fraught	slaughter	

Note that *au* → {æ} implies *gh* → {f} while *au* → {ɔ} implies *gh* → {ø}.

ei	→	{aɪ}	height, sleight		
ei	→	{e}	sleigh		
			freight	neighbor	
			inveigh	weigh	
ou	→	{ə}	clough, enough, rough, slough, sough, tough		
ou	→	{o}	borough, dough, furlough, thorough, though		
ou	→	{a}	hough		
ou	→	{u}	through		
ou	→	{au}	bough, slough, sough		
ou	→	{ɔ}	bought	ought	wrought
			cough	sought	
			fought	thought	
			nought	trough	

6. SECONDARY VOWEL PATTERNS

a. *Introduction*

The secondary vowel spellings differ from the primary vowel spellings in several important ways. First, they occur less frequently and have a more limited distribution. None appears commonly before geminate consonant clusters; some like *ai*, *au*, *ei*, and *eu* rarely occur in word-final position; others, like *ie* and *oa* rarely occur in word initial position. Second, while each primary vowel spelling has two basic correspondences, according to the graphemic environment and the morphemic composition of the word in which it occurs, each secondary vowel spelling generally has a single major correspondent. Third, the morphophonemic correspondences based upon the secondary vowel spellings tend not to alternate in quality with reduction in stress. Compare, for example, the first vowels in *neutral* : *neutrality*; *cause* : *causation* with those in *melody* : *melodious*; *potent* : *impotent*.

Historically, the secondary spellings also differ from the primary ones. Primary vowel spellings are found in the earliest English records; their correspondences can be traced through a complicated chain of sound changes from Old English to the present time. Most secondary vowel spellings, on the other hand, were introduced during the late Middle English period and consequently have been involved in considerably fewer sound changes. Correspondences for the secondary vowel spellings follow, divided into major and minor categories on the basis of frequency of occurrence in different English words.

b. *Correspondences*

ai/ay

Major Correspondences

{e} : b*ai*t, d*ay*, pl*ay*er, w*ai*t

Minor Correspondences

{ai} : *ai*sle, *ay*e, b*ay*ou, c*ay*enne
{i} : pl*ai*t, qu*ay*
{ɛ} : ag*ai*n, ag*ai*nst, s*ai*d
{æ} : pl*ai*d

au/aw

Major Correspondences

{ɔ} : *au*dience, cl*aw*, c*au*se

Minor Correspondences

{e} : g*au*ge
{æ} : *au*nt, dr*au*ght, l*au*gh
{o} : ch*au*ffeur, ch*au*vinist, h*au*tboy, m*au*ve
{au} : s*au*erkr*au*t, uml*au*t

ea

Major Correspondences

{i} : br*ea*ch, *ea*ch, r*ea*ch, t*ea*ch

Minor Correspondences

{e} : br*ea*k, gr*ea*t, st*ea*k, y*ea*
{ɛ} : (1) before *-l*, e.g., h*ea*lth, r*ea*lm, w*ea*lth
(2) before *-sure*, e.g., mea*sure*, plea*sure*, trea*sure*
(3) in the following words:

bread	spread	endeavor	pheasant
breadth	thread	feather	sweat
dead	tread	weather	sweater
dread	treadle	heaven	threat
head	breast	heavy	treachery
instead	breath	leather	weapon
meadow	deaf	leaven	weather
ready	death	peasant	

ee

Major Correspondences

{i} : bl*ee*d, *ee*l, absent*ee*

Minor Correspondences

{ɪ} : b*ee*n, br*ee*ches, cr*ee*k
{e} : matin*ee*, mel*ee*

ei/ey

Major Correspondences

{e} : ab*ey*ance, ob*ey*, r*ei*gn, v*ei*l

Minor Correspondences

{aɪ} : *ey*e, fahrenh*ei*t, g*ey*ser, gn*ei*ss, h*ei*ght, holst*ei*n kal*ei*doscope, sl*ei*ght, st*ei*n, wall*ey*e

{i} : caff*ei*n, c*ei*ling, conc*ei*t, conc*ei*ve, dec*ei*t, dec*ei*ve, *ei*ther, k*ey*, l*ei*sure, n*ei*ther, rec*ei*pt, rec*ei*ve, s*ei*ze, sh*ei*k

{ɛ} : h*ei*fer

eu/ew

Major Correspondences

{ju} : *ew*e, *eu*charist, n*eu*tron, p*ew*ter

Minor Correspondences

{o} : s*ew*, sh*ew*

ie

Major Correspondences

{ai} (in final position in monosyllabics): d*ie*, l*ie*, p*ie*, t*ie*

{ɪ} (in final position in polysyllabics): calor*ie*, coll*ie*, eer*ie*, mov*ie*

{i} (medial position): ach*ie*ve, d*ie*sel, n*ie*ce, y*ie*ld

Minor Correspondences

{e} : linger*ie*

{ɪ} : s*ie*ve

{ɛ} : fr*ie*nd

NOTE: *Allied*, *applied*, *dried*, etc., should be treated as *ally* + *ed*, *apply* + *ed*, *dry* + *ed*, etc. Likewise *bodied*, *candied*, *studied*, etc., should be treated as *body* + *ed*, *candy* + *ed*, *study* + *ed*, etc.

oa

Major Correspondences

{o} : appr*oa*ch, b*oa*st, g*oa*l, sh*oa*l

Minor Correspondences

{ɔ} : br*oa*d

oi/oy

Major Correspondences

{oɪ} : b*oy*, j*oi*n, l*oi*ter, *oy*ster

Minor Correspondences

{aɪ} : c*oy*ote
{ɪ} : cham*oi*s
{ə} : mademo*i*selle, porp*oi*se, tort*oi*se
{wa} : val*oi*s

oo

Major Correspondences

{u} : b*oo*t, br*oo*m, pr*oo*f, tyc*oo*n

Minor Correspondences

{ə} : bl*oo*d, fl*oo*d
{o} : br*oo*ch
{u} : p*oo*h
{ʊ} :

b*oo*k	f*oo*t	l*oo*k	sh*oo*k	w*oo*d
br*oo*k	fors*oo*k	mist*oo*k	s*oo*t	w*oo*l
c*oo*k	g*oo*d	n*oo*k	st*oo*d	
cr*oo*k	h*oo*k	r*oo*k	t*oo*k	

ou/ow

Major Correspondences

{au} : (initial and medial positions): ab*ou*nd, cr*ow*n, m*ou*ntain, *ow*l
{o} (final position): arr*ow*, b*ow*, gl*ow*, pill*ow*

Minor Correspondences

{ə} :

cl*ou*gh	d*ou*ble	sl*ou*gh	tr*ou*ble
c*ou*ntry	en*ou*gh	s*ou*gh	y*ou*ng
c*ou*ple	j*ou*st	t*ou*ch	
c*ou*sin	r*ou*gh	t*ou*gh	

{a} : h*ou*gh

{ɔ} : c*ou*gh, tr*ou*gh

{o} : b*ou*lder, b*ow*l, cantal*ou*p, m*ou*ld, m*ou*lt, *ow*e, *ow*n, p*ou*ltice, sh*ou*lder, sm*ou*lder, s*ou*l, thor*ou*gh

{ʊ} : b*ou*levard, c*ou*ld, f*ou*lard, sh*ou*ld, w*ou*ld

{u} :

acc*ou*ter	carib*ou*	gr*ou*p	r*ou*tine	tr*ou*badour
bay*ou*	c*ou*gar	rendezv*ou*s	s*ou*p	unc*ou*th
b*ou*doir	c*ou*pon	r*ou*ge	s*ou*venir	verm*ou*th
b*ou*le	cr*ou*p	r*ou*lette	st*ou*p	w*ou*nd
b*ou*quet	gh*ou*l	r*ou*te	t*ou*can	

{au} : all*ow*, br*ow*, c*ow*, end*ow*, h*ow*, m*ow*, n*ow*, pl*ow*, s*ow* pr*ow*, th*ou*, v*ow*

ui

Major Correspondences

{(j)u} : br*ui*se, n*ui*sance, purs*ui*t, s*ui*tor

Minor Correspondences

{ɪ} : bisc*ui*t, b*ui*ld, circ*ui*t

VIII

CONCLUSIONS

1. THE NATURE OF THE CURRENT ORTHOGRAPHY

a. *Base Forms and Compounds*

The spelling of the base form of a word tends to be phonemic — not in the one-letter one-sound system that has become the Holy Grail of many educators and linguists, but in a more graphemically economical fashion whereby position, environment, and overt markers allow the same symbol to perform several distinct functions, and whereby several symbols represent the same sound. (That *homo sapiens* is somehow more at ease with a one-letter one-sound system has often been assumed, but no evidence has ever been produced to substantiate this limitation on man's mental capacities).

The spelling of compounds and derivatives tends to be morphemic; the established graphemic form of the base is retained as much as possible, regardless of the phonemic alternations involved. Once, for example, the base form *melody* is established for /mέlədi/, it would be highly irregular to spell /məlódɪəs/ in any other way except with an initial segment *melodi-*. (The shift from *y* to *i* has no relation to the pronunciation; it stems from purely orthographic considerations). The orthographic preservation of morphemic identity is predicted on the assumption that the reader knows the phonemic alternations that accompany derivational and inflectional formations. The form *sign-* is spelled the same in *sign*, *signing*, *signal*, and *signify*, yet it has the different pronunciations

/sain-/ and /sɪgn-/. For the foreigner this is an obstacle towards learning to pronounce English from its spelling, but English spelling is geared for the convenience of the native speaker, not for the foreigner.

Even with these morphemic tendencies, the orthography employs numerous phonemic aids in forming derivational and inflectional forms. The doubling of the final consonant in forms like *can* : *canning*, *confer* : *conferred*, and the insertion of *k* in *picnicking* facilitate letter-to-sound conversion. The phonemic and the morphemic tendencies are equally strong; morphemic identity is seldom preserved at the expense of the more general phonemic patterns, and the general phonemic patterns, from all appearances, tend to preserve morphemic identity.

Rules for pronouncing English monosyllables are relatively simple; those for pronouncing polysyllabic but monomorphemic words, more complex; and those for polymorphemic words, the most complex. Spellings for monomorphemic words, while generally more phonemically based than those for polymorphemic words, still are not completely phonemic. Stress, form class, and phonotactics, among others, are conditioning factors. With polymorphemic words, even graphotactics becomes important. For example, the difference between the spelling *ie* in *believe* and in *applied* is readily apparent if one knows the graphotactical rules for changing final *y* to *i* before certain suffixes. Without a knowledge of this rule, however, one must view the *ie* spelling in *applied* as irregular.

b. *Loan Words and Homophones*

More irregular spellings in English are due to borrowings than to any other cause. Yet such borrowings cannot be classed as entirely irregular since their spellings often mark their foreign identities. Foreign spellings have been retained in English orthography since the Middle English period. For example, /č/ changed to /š/ in French in the thirteenth century although French orthography retained the *ch* spelling. At the time when the first French words with *ch* corresponding to /š/ were borrowed in English, the native orthography was still dynamic, yet English *sh* was not generally substituted for French *ch*. Some French spellings were altered, but seldom without prompting by a parallel alternation in French orthography.

In addition to leaving intact foreign spellings that contrasted with native ones, Middle and early Modern English scribes also tended to alter English spellings to reflect foreign origins. Thus, many *f*'s were replaced by *ph*'s and initial *h*'s added to exhibit French and Latin parentage. Occasionally an obsolete or foreign spelling was retained to differentiate forms with the same pronunciations.

This graphemic differentiation of homophones was noted as an essential feature of English orthography as early as the beginning of the seventeenth century. (See Hume, p. 19.) To what extent conscious efforts have been made to enforce this orthographic function is difficult to determine. Nevertheless, the number of homophones that are now differentiated graphemically is considerable. For an extensive list of such forms, see Robert Bridges, "On English Homophones", *SPE* Tract No. 2 (London, 1919).

2. SPELLING REFORM

A rational approach to spelling reform must recognize the various phonological, morphological and syntactical patterns in the current orthography, and must increase either the regularity of the existing patterns or the range of one group of patterns at the expense of others. To base spelling reform upon the argument that orthography should by nature be phonemic, morphemic, or anything else is both unrealistic and unsupportable. There is no valid basis, either diachronic or synchronic, for claiming that the current orthography should be anything in particular other than what it is. Some people may desire that it be phonemic or morphemic, but this is somewhat different from the claim that the orthography, by nature, should be that way.

To argue that the existing orthography is irregular and then to propose a phonemic alphabet for English as a cure is to present a *non-sequitur*. The existing irregularities are in the syntactic and morphological patterns as much as in the phonological ones, so a phonemic alphabet, while presumably correcting the phonological deviations, creates even greater irregularities in the other patterning systems.

Certain spelling changes can be made without altering the basis of the existing system, while others require entirely new orthographic principles. Eliminating the silent letters in *debt*, *doubt*, and *subtle*, for example, would make the current system more systematic. But to spell the first vowel in both *sane* and *sanity* with different letters would change a basic morphological pattern.

Even in the attempts to institute a phonemic system, varying degrees of change are required. One letter for one sound proposals would completely alter the existing system. The same results, obtained through an extension of the current phonemic patterns like the final *e* pattern and consonant gemination, coupled with a few new letters, could cause a much smaller change, and would preserve a large number of the morphemic patterns.

3. THE TEACHING OF READING

a. *Regular and Irregular Correspondences*

In view of the foregoing conclusions, some notice must be given to the concept 'regular spelling-to-sound correspondences' which is paraded quite frequently through the current literature on reading and orthography. Educators claim that the earliest reading instruction should be built around such correspondences. Psychologists report the results on children of various feedings of these entities, and linguists have been prone to dismiss the entire orthographic system with a single flap of the regular-irregular banner. Since prior to the past few years no extensive analysis of the current orthography has been available, it is difficult to imagine what the concept of regularity was based upon other than upon a simple letter-to-sound view. Rather than thrash through the few definitions which have been offered, I intend to analyze anew this concept, based upon the material presented in this book.

Regularity implies, in some sense, a numerical predominance of one event over others. To claim that by some reckoning the correspondence $a \rightarrow b$ is regular requires that clearly definable entities be counted. Exactly what criterion level must be reached to have regularity cannot and need not be answered. Certainly, if $a \rightarrow b$ occurs in 99 percent of all correspondences for *a*, then it would be labeled as regular. But if it occurs in 51 percent, or 60, or 70, or even 80 percent, an arbitrary decision would have to be made. But this is not a problem unique to spelling-to-sound correspondences, but to the definition of the term regular, and need not be a concern at present.

The true problem faced here is in deciding what to count. *c*, for example, corresponds to /k/ in approximately 74 percent of its correspondences, to /s/ in approximately 22 percent, and to /š/ in approximately 4 percent. In addition, it corresponds to /č/ in two different words. Suppose that we had arbitrarily decided on a criterion level of 73 percent for regularity. Then, *c* → /k/ would be regular and all the other correspondences would be irregular. But this is patently absurd since it is clear that *c* corresponds to /k/ in one set of environments, to /s/ in a different set, and to /š/ in a totally different set. That is, by considering environment alone, three of the four correspondences for *c*, accounting for all words containing *c* except two, become regular.

If, however, environment is accepted as a variable in the determination of regularity, the problem then becomes "what is an admissable environment?" Consider as a starting point the problem of palatalization which was discussed earlier. To predict palatalization, the word stress pattern must be known. For example, medial *d* before *u* corresponds to /d/ in about 60 percent of the words in which this sequence occurs and to /ǰ/ in the remaining occurrences. Without considering stress, d → /ǰ/ would be classed as irregular. If, however, stress is considered as part of the environment for *d*, then both *d*→/d/ and *d*→/ǰ/ are regular.

Morphology is also significant, especially for the designation of spelling units. Are, for example, the correspondences for medial *t* and *h* in *hothouse* to be considered irregular correspondences for the unit *th* or regular correspondences for the separate units *t* and *h*? In all of these examples the question of regularity cannot be resolved adequately without reference to the underlying patterns of the orthography. But considerations of such patterns do not automatically determine regularity. Before unstressed /ju/, /d/ palatalizes, as do /t/, /s/ and /z/, e.g., *credulous, creature, erasure* (also -ž-), and *azure*. Before unstressed /ɪ/ or /j/ plus vowel, however, /d/ tends not to palatalize, but /t/, /s/ and /z/ do. Thus, *custodian, medial, radiance*, but *bastion, appreciate, abrasion*. In relation to its immediate environment *d* regularly corresponds to /d/ before unstressed *i* plus vowel, but in relation to the more general pattern of palatalization, *d* is irregular here. These problems concern not only regularity, but also the concept of simplicity. A description of spelling-to-sound correspondences that considers only direct letter-to-sound relationships without regard to morphology or stress is certainly simpler than the model presented in this paper, and is, in some sense correct, yet linguistically it is inadequate since it fails to describe many phenomena which bear upon spelling-to-sound relationships. In other words, simplicity is secondary to linguistic adequacy, which implies that no consideration of simplicity is meaningful until all relevant phenomena are described. Then, simplicity enters only if more than one explanation is adequate for all the data.

Regularity occupies a position similar in importance to that of simplicity. Until we have discovered all existing patterns we cannot be sure that any one pattern is regular or irregular; that is, until all countable entities (patterns) are uncovered, counting is meaningless. There are obviously points in an investigation where supportable statements about regularity and simplicity can be made, but all such statements must be tentative. Whether or not such statements ever become definite in an investigation of natural language is a question beyond the scope of this paper.

In the present study the primary goal has been to discover and describe the underlying patterns of the current orthography. The discovery of patterns is itself based upon predictability so that ultimately the regular spelling-to-sound correspondences are those that are predictable from orthographic patterns. In the complete description, unpredictable spelling-to-sound correspondences must be overtly marked so that predictable correspondences, which are the majority, will be the residue. The alternative to this procedure is to list for each pattern all words which fit the pattern, so that the residue would consist of words with irregular correspondences. But this is, by definition, more complex than the first procedure since more words must be listed. In addition, this approach requires that words added to English be listed under each regular pattern which they contain, rather than under the irregular patterns, which tend to be in the minority.

In place of the categories, REGULAR, and IRREGULAR, the following classification scheme for spelling-to-sound patterns is offered:

I. Predictable: patterns that can be predicted upon the basis of regular graphemic, morphemic or phonemic features of the words or sentences in which they occur.
   A. Invariant: patterns which admit no (or very few) variations or exceptions.
   B. Variant: patterns which have predictable variations or exceptions. (Variant patterns could be divided further on the basis of the features needed to predict each pattern).

II. Unpredictable: all patterns which do not fit into I above.
   A. Affix-aided: patterns which could be derived by relating the word to one of its prefixed or suffixed forms, e.g., *sign-signal.*
   B. High-frequency: occurs frequently (frequent enough to allow an association group to be profitably employed in teaching).
   C. Low-frequency: occurs too infrequently to merit the formation of an association group.

The importance of this classification for the teaching of reading is that it separates patterns according to the pedagogy which can be employed to teach them. All predictable patterns could be taught by rules — that is, through reasoning — although this may not be the best technique for some of them. Furthermore, the differences between the invariant and variant predictable patterns can be related to the teaching of a set for invariance as against teaching a set for variance. Presenting all the invariant patterns before introducing any of the variant ones may interfere with the teaching of the latter through reinforcement of this set for invariance.

In the unpredictable class, the low-frequency patterns should not be presented as letter-sound or sound-letter patterns since this may encourage transfer to inappropriate situations. The high-frequency patterns cannot, in a strict sense, be transferred either, since there is no way to predict where they apply. However, by associating the words in which a particular pattern occurs, an extra measure of learning efficiency might be gained.

From this classification for letter-sound and sound-letter patterns, a three-fold classification for reading and spelling words is derived. (The word groups for reading will rarely be the same as those for spelling).

Class I-Transfer words: Words which contain predictable patterns. The patterns in these words can be transferred to the pronunciation (or spelling) of other words in which the same spellings (or pronunciations) occur.

Class II-Association words: Words grouped according to frequently occurring, but unpredictable patterns.

Class III-Isolated words: Words which should be handled as whole words to inhibit transfer of unpredictable, low frequency patterns.

b. *Pedagogy*

English spelling-to-sound correspondences can be described in terms of patterns of graphemic, morphemic, syntactic, and phonotactical processes. With these patterns a complete model can be constructed for relating spelling-to-sound, a model from which the rules needed to predict the pronunciation of any word can be found. What relationship this model has to the reading process of literates or to the teaching of reading is at present unknown. It is safe to predict that many of the patterns in the model have no counterparts in reading habits, yet this does not say that there is no relationship between the linguistic constructs and the reading process. As a minimum it can be assumed that the classification scheme for spelling-to-sound patterns presented above could be used as a basis for the selection of words for the teaching of reading. How the frequency of occurrence of various words in running text is to be weighed in the selection of reading words is a problem for the psychologists and educators to decide.

Another area in which the linguistic patterns could be helpful is in the selection of the age level for introducing various correspondences. If it is assumed that at the time a child is first taught to read he has mastered all of the patterns of English which are important for reading, then one could safely introduce any existing spelling-to-sound correspondence. But it is doubtful that this is true. While a first grade child may know most or all of the phonology and syntax of English, he probably lacks some of the morphophonemics. Since experimental evidence is lacking for determining the age of comprehension (and production) of much of the morphophonemics of English, consideration should be given to the language features upon which various correspondences are based. To introduce, for example, the alternation of the voiced velar stop with zero in *strong/stronger* before the child recognizes or produces such an alternation, is probably not desirable. Many of the patterns discussed in this paper may have little bearing upon the initial stages of reading instruction, but might be helpful in later stages where morphology and syntax become more important. The various pronunciations of final *-ate* and initial *th-* are examples of such patterns.

In the translation from spelling-to-sound, words must in some sense be scanned. Whether the scanning is through eye movements or cognitive processes is immaterial. What is important is that except where whole words are recognized, a sequence of units within the word is observed in the translation process. The relevance of this to the teaching of reading is in the instructions given to a child who is first learning to read. Should he be told to scan left to right, letter by letter, pronouncing as he goes, or is there a more efficient scheme? In the first place, a person who attempts to scan left to right, letter by letter, pronouncing as he goes, could not correctly read most English words. Many of the English spelling-to-sound patterns require, at a minimum, a knowledge of succeeding graphemic units. How, for example, is initial *e*- to be pronounced if the following units are not known (cf. *erb*, *ear*, *ewer*, *eight*)? This is just the beginning of the problem. In some patterns, the entire word must be seen — and this is true of almost all polysyllabic words since stress patterns are significant for vowel quality. The implication here is that single pass left-to-right scanning is unproductive except for some monosyllabic words. Whether the reader experiments with several stress patterns and then selects the most English-like one or whether he utilizes some other scheme is not known, but should be determined.

BIBLIOGRAPHY

Bazell, Charles E., "The Grapheme", *Litera* 3 (1956), 43.

Bethel, John P., ed., *Webster's New Collegiate Dictionary*, 2d ed. (Springfield, Mass., 1956).

Bloomfield, Leonard, *Language* (New York, 1933).

——, "Linguistics and Reading", *The Elementary English Review* XIX (1942), 125-30, 183-86.

——, and Barnhart, Clarence K., *Let's Read: a Linguistic Approach* (Detroit, 1961).

Bopp, F., *Uber das Konjugationssystem der Sanskritsprache* (Frankfurt am Main, 1916).

Bradley, Henry, "On the Relations between Spoken and Written Language with Special Reference to English", *British Academy* 6 (1914), 211-32.

Bridges, Robert, "On English Homophones", *SPE* Tract No. 2 (London, 1919).

Brown, Goold, *The Grammar of English Grammars*, 4th ed. (New York, 1859).

Bullokar, William, *Booke at Large, for the Amendment of Orthographie for English Speech* (London, 1580).

Burchfield, R. W., "The Language and Orthography of the Ormulum MS", *Trans. Phil. Soc.* (1956), 56-87.

Butler, Charles, *The English Grammar* (Oxford, 1634). Re-issued with an introduction by Albert Eichler (Halle, 1910).

Craigie, William A., *English Spelling, Its Rules and Reasons* (New York, 1927).

—— "Some Anomalies of Spelling", *SPE* Tract No. 59 (London, 1942).

——, "The Critique of Pure English from Caxton to Smollett", *SPE* Tract No. 65 (London, 1946).

Danielson, Bror, *John Hart's Works on Orthography and Pronunciation* (Stockholm, 1955).

Dobson, Eric J., *English Pronunciation 1500-1700*, 2 vols. (Oxford, 1957).

Downing, John, "Pitman's Initial Teaching Alphabet", Paper read at the conference on perceptual and linguistic aspects of reading (Stanford, California, October 31, 1963).

Edgerton, William F., "Ideograms in English Writing", *Lg.* 17 (1941), 148-50.

Ellis, Alexander ., "On the Diphthong 'oy'", *Trans. Phil. Soc.* (1867), Supp. I, pp. 53-66.

Elphinston, James, *On the English Language* (London, 1796).

Ewert, Alfred, *The French Language* (London, 1933).
Flom, George T., "Studies in Scandinavian Paleography", *JEGP* 14 (1915), 530-43.
Francis, W. Nelson, *The Structure of American English* (New York, 1958).
Franklin, Benjamin, "A Scheme for a New Alphabet and Reformed Mode of Spelling", in John Bigelow, ed. *The Works of Benjamin Franklin*, 12 vols. (New York, 1904). Vol. V, pp. 30-37.
Fries, Charles C., *The Teaching of English* (Ann Arbor, 1949).
——, *Linguistics and Reading* (New York, 1963).
Gaines, H. F., *Cryptanalysis* (New York, 1939).
Gibson, E. J., *et al.*, "An Analysis of Critical Features of Letters, Tested by a Confusion Matrix" in Harry Levin, ed., *A Basic Research Program on Reading* (Cornell University, 1963).
Gill, Alexander, *Logonomia Anglica* (London, 1619).
Gimson, A. C., *An Introduction to the Pronunciation of English* (New York, 1962).
Gleason, H. A., Jr., *An Introduction to Descriptive Linguistics* (New York, 1961).
Grimm, J., *Deutsche Grammatik* (Gottingen, 1819-1837).
Hall, Rob ert., r., *Linguistics and your Language* (Garden City, 1960).
——, *Sound and Spelling in English* (Philadelphia, 1961).
——, "Graphemics and Linguistics", Proceedings of 1962 annual spring meeting of the American Ethnological Society, pp. 53-59.
Haugen, Einar, *First Grammatical Treatise: the Earliest Germanic Philology*, Language monogram No. 25 (Baltimore, 1950).
——, "Directions in Modern Linguistics", *Lg.* 27 (1951), 211-22.
Hockett, Charles F., *A Course in Modern Linguistics* (New York, 1958).
——, "Analysis of Graphic Monosyllables", Harry Levin, *et al. A Basic Research Program on Reading* (Cornell University, 1963).
Holmberg, Borje, *James Douglas on English Pronunciation c. 1740.* Lund studies in English XXVI (Lund, 1956).
Hume, Alexander, *Of the Orthographie and Congruitie of the Britian Tongue.* Edited with an introduction by Henry B. Wheatley, *EETS* publication No. 5 (London, 1865).
Jespersen, Otto H., *A Modern English Grammar on Historical Principles.* 7 vols. (Heidelberg, 1909-1949).
——, *Essentials of English Grammar* (New York, 1933).
Jones, D., *Outline of English Phonetics*, 3rd ed. (Leipzig, 1932).
Jonson, Ben, *The English Grammar* (London, 1634).
Kenyon, John S., *American Pronunciation*, 9th ed. (Ann Arbor, 1943).
Kenyon, John S., and Knott, Thomas, *A Pronuncing Dictionary of American English* (Springfield, Mass., 1951).
Kingdon, Roger, *The Groundwork of English Stress* (London, 1958).
Kittredge, George L., "Some Landmarks in the History of English Grammars", Text-book bulletin for schools and colleges, 1906 (New York).
Krapp, G. P., *The Pronunciation of Standard English in America* (New York, 1919).

Kurath, Hans, "The Loss of Long Consonants and the Rise of Voiced Fricatives in Middle English", *Lg.* 32 (1956), 435-45.

——, *A Phonology and Prosody of Modern English* (Ann Arbor, 1964).

——, and McDavid, Raven I., Jr., *The Pronunciation of English in the Atlantic States* (Ann Arbor, 1961).

Lehiste, Ilse, *Accoustical Characteristics of Selected English Consonants*, IJAL publication No. 34 (Bloomington, 1964).

Levin, Harry, *et al.*, *A Basic Research Program on Reading*, Final report, Cooperative research project No. 639 (Cornell University, 1963).

——, editor, *Project Literacy Reports* (Ithaca, 1964-67).

Lily, William, *Short Introduction of Grammar* (London, 1549).

Lounsbury, Thomas R., *English Spelling and Spelling Reform* (New York, 1909).

McIntosh, Angus, "The Analysis of Written Middle English" *Trans. Phil. Soc.* (1956), 26-55.

McLaughlin, John C., *A Graphemic-Phonemic Study of a Middle English Manuscript* (The Hague, 1963).

Marchand, Hans, *The Categories and Types of Present-Day English Word-Formation* (Wiesbaden, 1960).

Marckwardt, Albert H., "Origin and Extension of the Voiceless Preterit and the Past Participle Inflections of the English Irregular Weak Verb Conjugations", University of Michigan Publications: *Essays and studies in English and comparative literature*, Vol. XIII, pp. 151-328 (Ann Arbor, 1935).

Middle English Dictionary. Edited by Hans Kurath (Ann Arbor, 1954).

Mulcaster, Richard, *The First Part of the Elementarie Which Entreateth Chefelie of the Right Writing of Our English Tung* [1582] Edited with an introduction by E. T. Campagnac (Oxford, 1925).

Newman, Stanley S., "English Suffixation: A Descriptive Approach", *Word* 4 (1948), 24-36.

The Oxford English Dictionary, 12 vols. Edited by James A. H. Murray, *et al.* Corrected re-issue (Oxford, 1933).

Paul, H., *Prinzipien der Sprachgeschichte* (Halle, 1880).

Peterson, Gordon E. and Lehiste, Ilse, "Duration of Syllable Nuclei", *JASA*, 32 (1960), 693-703.

Pitman, Isaac J., "Learning to Read: an Experiment", *Journal of the Royal Society of Arts*, 109 (1961), 149-180.

Pratt, Fletcher, *Secret and Urgent; the Story of Codes and Ciphers* (Indianapolis, 1939).

Pulgram, Ernst, "Phoneme and Grapheme: a Parallel", *Word* 7 (1951), 15-20.

——, "Graphic and Phonic Systems: Figurae and Signs", *Word* 21 (1965), 208-224.

Rask, R. K., *Undersøgelse om det Nordiske Eller Islandske Sprogs Oprindelse* (Copenhagen, 1818).

Saussure, Ferdinand de, *Cours de linguistique générale* (Paris, 1916). Translated by Wade Baskin, *Course in General Linguistics* (New York, 1959).

Stetson, Raymond H., "The Phoneme and the Grapheme", *Mélanges -de linguistique et de phonologie offerts à Jacq. van Ginneken* (Paris, 1937), 353-56.

Sweet, Henry, "The History of the 'th' in English", *Trans. Phil. Soc.* (1868-1869), 272-88.
——, *A History of English Sounds from the Earliest Period* (Oxford, 1888).
Thorndike, Edward L., *The Teaching of English Suffixes* (New York, 1941).
——, *Thorndike-Century Senior Dictionary* (New York, 1941).
Vachek, Josef, "Some Remarks on Writing and Phonetic Transcription", *Acta Linguistica* 5 (1945-1949), 86-93.
——, "Two Chapters on Written English", *Brno Studies in English*, Vol. 1 (Praha, 1959).
——, "On the Interplay of External and Internal Factors in the Development of Language", *Lingua* 11 (1962), 433-48.
Venezky, Richard L., "A Computer Program for Deriving Spelling to Sound Correlations", Masters thesis (Cornell University, 1962). Published in part in Harry Levin, *et al.* *A Basic Research Program on Reading* (Cornell University, 1963).
——, "A Study of English Spelling-to-Sound Correspondences on Historical Principles". Unpublished doctoral dissertation (Stanford University, 1965).
——, "English Orthography: its Graphical Structure and its Relation to Sound", *Reading Research Quarterly*, II, 75-106 (Spring, 1967).
——, "Reading: Grapheme-Phoneme Relationships", *Education* 87 (1967), 519-24.
——, "The Basis of English Orthography", *Acta Linguistica* 10 (1967), 145-59.
——, and Weir, Ruth H., *A Study of Selected Spelling-to-Sound Correspondence Patterns*, Final report, Co-operative Research Project No. 3090 (Stanford, 1966).
Waldo, George S., "The Significance of Accentuation in English Words", *Proceedings of the Ninth International Congress of Linguists* (The Hague, 1965), 204-10.
Webster, Noah, *An American Dictionary of the English Language*. Revised and enlarged by Chauncey A. Goodrich (Springfield, Mass., 1852).
Webster's New Collegiate Dictionary. Edited by John P. Bethel, 2nd ed. (Springfield, Mass., 1956).
Webster's Third New International Dictionary. Edited by Phillip B. Gove (Springfield, Mass., 1963).
Weir, Ruth H., "Formulation of Grapheme-Phoneme Correspondence Rules to Aid in the Teaching of Reading", Final report, Co-operative Research Project No. S-039 (Stanford, 1964).
——, and Venezky, Richard L., "Rules to Aid in the Teaching of Reading", Final report, Co-operative Research Project No. 2584 (Stanford, 1965).
Whitney, William D., *Language and the Study of Language* (New York, 1967).
Wijk, Axel, *Rules of Pronunciation for the English Language* (London, 1966).
Zachrisson, Robert E., *Anglic, a New Agreed Simplified English Spelling* (Uppsala, 1930).
——, "Four Hundred Years of English Spelling Reform", *Studia Neophilologica* 4 (1931), 1-69.

INDEX OF TERMS

WORD INDEX

E

INDEX OF NAMES

29. PUNYA SLOKA RAY: Language Standardization: Studies in Prescriptive Linguistics. 1963. 159 pp. Gld. 20.—
30. PAUL L. GARVIN: On Linguistic Method: Selected Papers. 1964. 158 pp. Gld. 16.—
31. LÁSZLÓ ANTAL: Content, Meaning and, Understanding. 1964. 63 pp. Gld. 9.50
32. GEORGES MOUNIN: La machine à traduire: Histoire des problèmes linguistiques. 1964. 209 pp. Gld. 32.—
33. ROBERT E. LONGACRE: Grammar Discovery Procedure: A Field Manual. 1964. 162 pp. Gld. 12.—
34. WILLIAM S. COOPER: Set Theory and Syntactic Description. 1964. 52 pp. Gld. 9.50
35. LUIS J. PRIETO: Principes de noologie: Fondements de la théorie fonctionnelle du signifié. Préface d'André Martinet. 1964. 130 pp., 36 figs. Gld. 21.—
36. SEYMOUR CHATMAN: A Theory of Meter. 1965. 229 pp., many graphs, 2 plates. Gld. 23.—
37. WAYNE TOSH: Syntactic Translation. 1965. 162 pp., 58 figs. Gld. 23.—
38. NOAM CHOMSKY: Current Issues in Linguistic Theory. 1964. 119 pp. Gld. 12.—
39. D. CRYSTAL and R. QUIRK: Systems of Prosodic and Paralinguistic Features in English. 1964. 94 pp., 16 plates. Gld. 14.—
40. FERENC PAPP: Mathematical Linguistics in the Soviet Union. 1966. 165 pp. Gld. 24.—
41. S. K. ŠAUMJAN: Problems of Theoretical Phonology. 1968. 224 pp. figs. Gld. 26.—
42. MILKA IVIĆ: Trends in Linguistics. Translated by Muriel Heppell. 1965. 260 pp. Gld. 28.—
43. ISTVÁN FODOR: The Rate of Linguistic Change: Limits of the Application of Mathematical Methods in Linguistics. 1965. 85 pp., some figs. Gld. 13.—
44. THEODORE M. DRANGE: Type Crossings: Sentential Meaninglessness in the Border Area of Linguistics and Philosophy. 1966. 218 pp. Gld. 23.—
45. WARREN H. FAY: Temporal Sequence in the Perception of Speech. 1966. 126 pp., 29 figs. Gld. 19.50
46. A. CAPELL: Studies in Socio-Linguistics. 1966. 167 pp., 2 tables. Gld. 22.—
47. BOWMAN CLARKE: Language and Natural Theology. 1966. 181 pp. Gld. 26.—
49. SAMUEL ABRAHAM and FERENC KIEFER: A Theory of Structural Semantics. 1966. 98 pp., 20 figs. Gld. 15.—
50. ROBERT J. SCHOLES: Phonotactic Grammatically. 1966. 117 pp., many figs. Gld. 15.—
51. HOWARD R. POLLIO: The Structural Basis of Word Association Behavior. 1966. 96 pp., 4 folding tables, 8 pp. graphs, figs. Gld. 16.—

52. JEFFREY ELLIS: Towards & General Comparative Linguistics. 1966. 170 pp. Gld. 22.—
54. RANDOLPH QUIRK and JAN SVARTVIK: Investigating Linguistic Acceptability. 1966. 118 pp., 14 figs., 4 tables. Gld. 15.—
55. THOMAS A. SEBEOK (ED.): Selected Writings of Gyula Laziczius. 1966. 226 pp. Gld. 26.—
56. NOAM CHOMSKY: Topics in the Theory of Generative Grammar. 1966. 96 pp. Gld. 12.—
58. LOUIS G. HELLER and JAMES MACRIS: Parametric Linguistics. 1967. 80 pp., 23 tables. Gld. 10.—
59. JOSEPH H. GREENBERG: Language Universals: With Special Reference to Feature Hierarchies. 1966. 89 pp. Gld. 18.—
60. CHARLES F. HOCKETT: Language, Mathematics, and Linguistics. 1967. 244 pp., figs. Gld. 21.—
62. B. USPENSKY: Principles of Structural Typology. 1968. 80 pp. Gld. 14.—
63. V. Z. PANFILOV: Grammar and Logic. 1968. 106 pp. Gld. 16.—
64. JAMES C. MORRISON: Meaning and Truth in Wittgenstein's Tractatus. 1968. 148 pp. Gld. 18.—
65. ROGER L. BROWN: Wilhelm von Humboldt's Conception of Linguistic Relativity. 1967. 132 pp. Gld. 16.—
66. EUGENE J. BRIERE: A Psycholinguistic Study of Phonological Interference. 1968. 84 pp. Gld. 12.—
67. ROBERT L. MILLER: The Linguistic Relativity Principle and New Humboldtian Ethnolinguistics: A History and Appraisal. 1968. 127 pp. Gld. 16.—
69. I. M. SCHLESINGER: Sentence Structure and the Reading Process. 1968. 172 pp. Gld. 18.—
70. A. ORTIZ and E. ZIERER: Set Theory and Linguistics. 1968. 64 pp. Gld. 10.—
71. HANS-HEINRICH LIEB: Communication Complexes and Their Stages. 1968. 140 pp. Gld. 17.—
72. ROMAN JAKOBSON: Child Language, Aphasia and Phonological Universals. 1968. 104 pp. Gld. 12.—
73. CHARLES F. HOCKETT: The State of the Art. 1968. 124 pp. Gld. 14.—
74. A. JUILLAND and HANS-HEINRICH LIEB: "Klasse" und "Klassifikation" in der Sprachwissenschaft. 1968. 75 pp. Gld. 13.—
75. JIŘÍ KRÁMSKÝ: The Word as a Linguistic Unit. 82 pp. Gld. 12.—
76. URSULA OOMEN: Automatische Syntaktische Analyse. 1968. 84 pp. Gld. 16.—

MOUTON · PUBLISHERS · THE HAGUE